Harvard Legal Essays

WRITTEN IN HONOR OF AND PRESENTED TO

JOSEPH HENRY BEALE

AND

SAMUEL WILLISTON

A LIST OF LEGAL TREATISES PRINTED IN THE BRITISH COLONIES AND THE AMERICAN STATES BEFORE 1801

ELDON REVARE JAMES

THE LAWBOOK EXCHANGE, LTD.
Union, New Jersey
2002

ISBN-13: 978-1-58477-143-2
ISBN-10: 1-58477-143-7

Third printing 2006

Printed in the United States of America on acid-free paper

THE LAWBOOK EXCHANGE, LTD.
33 Terminal Avenue
Clark, New Jersey 07066-1321

Please see our website for a selection of our other publications and fine facsimile reprints of classic works of legal history:
www.lawbookexchange.com

Library of Congress Cataloging-in-Publication Data

James, Eldon R. (Eldon Revare), 1875-1949.
A list of legal treatises printed in the British colonies and the American states before
1801 / Eldon Revare James.
p. cm.
Originally published: Cambridge, Mass.: Harvard University Press, 1934.
ISBN 1-58477-143-7 (cloth: alk. paper)
1. Law—United States—Bibliography. 2. Law—Great Britain—Bibliography. I. Title.

KF1 .J36 2001
016.34973—dc21

00-067773

Harvard Legal Essays

WRITTEN IN HONOR OF AND PRESENTED TO

JOSEPH HENRY BEALE

AND

SAMUEL WILLISTON

A LIST OF LEGAL TREATISES PRINTED IN THE BRITISH COLONIES AND THE AMERICAN STATES BEFORE 1801

ELDON REVARE JAMES

Cambridge, Massachusetts

HARVARD UNIVERSITY PRESS

1934

A LIST OF LEGAL TREATISES PRINTED IN THE BRITISH COLONIES AND THE AMERICAN STATES BEFORE 1801

ELDON REVARE JAMES

IN THE hundred years between the publication in 1687 of William Penn's gleanings from Lord Coke and the issuance of the American editions of Buller's Nisi Prius and Gilbert's Evidence in 1788, not a single book that could be called a treatise intended for the use of professional lawyers was published in the British Colonies and the American States. All of the books within this period which by any stretch of definition might be regarded as legal treatises were for the use of laymen. The merchant, the farmer, the artisan, might at any time be called upon to serve as a justice of the peace, or even, in some colonies and states, in a higher judicial capacity. As lawyers were not numerous, the layman frequently and perhaps generally drafted his own instruments, contracts, deeds, and wills, without professional assistance. He was also called upon frequently to serve as a juryman. Practically all of these books were designed to assist him in the performance of his judicial and other public duties, and to enable him to satisfy legal requirements in the everyday matters of business and affairs.

In addition to these law books for laymen, a number of books and pamphlets of a political nature were issued. Although they may contain material of legal value, they can hardly be called legal treatises. Therefore the tract attributed to Lord Somers, The Judgment of Whole Kingdoms, has been omitted. For similar reasons, The Federalist and the other publications concerned with the question of the adoption of the Federal Constitution, and also the literature dealing with the controversy over the Jay Treaty, such as The American Remembrancer, have not been included in the list. Briefs and printed arguments, also, of which there are a few before 1801, have not been listed. While interesting and important, they are not legal treatises.

As it is his exclusions that cause him the most concern, the writer has no apology to offer for including works of a criminological character. They are not numerous, but show that eighteenth-century American publishers were convinced that a sufficient interest in such matters existed to justify the financial risks involved.

No bibliographical list, and particularly one in a new field, can ever be regarded as complete and final. This list, therefore, is a tentative one, and although an attempt has been made through the search of available library catalogues and bibliographies, and through the insistent pursuit of generous librarians and others, to make it as complete as possible, it is not believed that everything has been found. Unlisted titles and editions will undoubtedly be brought to light. Not the least of the trials of the bibliographer is that he can never be sure that he has found everything.

All books for which no authority is given are to be found in the Library of the Harvard Law School.*

1687

1. The Excellent Priviledge of / Liberty & Property / being the / Birth-right / Of the Free-born Subjects of England. / Containing / I. Magna Charta, with a learned Comment

* Grateful acknowledgment is made of the generous assistance rendered by Mr. John T. Vance, Library of Congress; Mr. Lawrence C. Wroth, John Carter Brown Library; Mr. Clarence S. Brigham and Mr. R. W. G. Vail, American Antiquarian Society; Mr. H. M. Lydenberg and Mr. K. D. Metcalf, New York Public Library; Miss Frances D. Lyon, New York State Library; Mr. George S. Godard, Connecticut State Library; Mr. Julius H. Tuttle, Massachusetts Historical Society; Miss Elinor Gregory, Boston Athenaeum; Miss Mary L. Thornton, Univ. of North Carolina; Mr. Otis G. Hammond, New Hampshire Historical Society; the Honorable William E. Marvin, Portsmouth, N. H.; and the Honorable William H. Sawyer, Chief Justice of the Superior Court of New Hampshire. I wish also to express my thanks to my colleague, Mr. Robert B. Anderson, of the Harvard Law School Library, who has at all times placed at my disposal his great knowledge in the field of legal bibliography.

Extensive use has been made of American Bibliography by Charles Evans and The Issues of the Press in Pennsylvania, 1685–1784, by Charles R. Hildeburn, cited hereafter, respectively, as Evans and Hildeburn.

upon / it. / II. The Confirmation of the Charters of the Li- / berties of England and of the Forrest, made in / the 35th year of Edward the First. / III. A Statute made the 34 Edw. I. commonly / called De Tallageo non Concedendo; wherein all / Fundamental Laws, Liberties and Customs are / confirmed. With a Comment upon it. / IV. An abstract of the Pattent granted by the / King to William Penn and his Heirs and As- / signs for the Province of Pennsilvania. / V. And Lastly, The Charter of Liberties granted by the said William Penn to the Free-men and / Inhabitants of the Province of Pennsilvania and / Territories thereunto annexed, In America. / Major Haereditas venit unicunq; nostrum a / Jure & Legibus, quam a Parentibus. / [1687.] Pages, (8), 63. Evans, 433. Written by William Penn, it was printed by William Bradford in Philadelphia in 1687. Only one copy is recorded, that in the Library of the Meeting for Sufferings in Philadelphia. It was reproduced in facsimile in 155 copies by the Philobiblon Club, Philadelphia, 1897. The Comment is largely taken from Coke's Second Institute.

1693

2. The Englishman's right: a dialogue between a barrister-at-law, and a jury-man; plainly setting forth the antiquity, the excellent designed use, and the office and just privileges of juries by the Laws of England. By Sir John Hawles. Boston: Printed by Benjamin Harris. 1693. 8vo. Evans, 639.*

1710

3. The / Constables Pocket-Book: / or, a / Dialogue / Between an / Old Constable & a New, / Being a Guide, / In their Keeping the Peace, &c. / In Serving all Warrants. / Observing Orders of Courts. / Summoning Town-Officers, and / Town-Meetings. / Collecting Rates and Assessments.

* Lex Mercatoria by Cotton Mather, printed in Boston, 1705, Evans, 1215, which is listed in Warren's History of the American Bar, p. 158, as one of the first seven law books printed in the British Colonies, is not a law book but a sermon upon the ethical duties of merchants.

/ Serving Writs, Summons, Executions. / How to make Returns of all Writs / and Warrants. / Forms of Bail — Bonds, &c. / An Account of all Lawful Fees. / By N[icholas]. B[oone]. a late Constable in the / Town of Boston, N. E. / Boston: Printed for Nicholas Boone, at his Shop / at the Sign of the Bible in Corn-hill, 1710. Pages, 70. 14 cm.

1716

4. Lex Parliamentaria: / or, a / Treatise / of the / Law and Custom / of the / Parliaments / of / England. / By G. P[etyt]. Esq; / Licenced December 6. 1689 / London Printed, and Reprinted in New-York / and Sold by William and Andrew Bradford / in New-York and Philadelphia, 1716. / Pages, (6), 184. 15 cm.

1721

5. English Liberties, / or the / Free-born Subjects' Inheritance; / containing / Magna Charta, Charta de Foresta, / The Statute De Tallagio non concedendo, / The Habeas Corpus Act, and several o- / ther Statutes, with Comments on each / of them. / Likewise / The Proceedings in Appeals of Murder: Of / Ship-Money; Of Tonnage and Poundage. Of Par- / liaments, and the Qualification and Choice of / Members: Of the Three Estates, and of the Set- / tlement of the Crown by Parliament. / Together with / A short History of the Succession, not by any Here- / ditary Right: Also a Declaration of the Liberties of the / Subject: And of the Oath of Allegiance and Supremacy. / The Petition of Right; with a short but impartial re- / lation of the Difference between K. Charles I and the / Long Parliament, concerning the Prerogative of the King, / the Liberties of the Subject, and the Rise of the Civil / Wars. Of Trials by Juries and of the Qualifications / of Jurors; their Punishment for Misbehaviour, and of / Challenges to them. / Lastly, / Of Justices of the Peace, Coroners, Constables, / Churchwardens, Overseers of the Poor, Surveyors of / the Highways, &c. With many Law-Cases through- / out the

Whole. / Compiled first by Henry Care, and contiued [*sic*], with / large Additions, by W. N[elson]. of the Middle-Temple, Esq; / The Fifth Edition. / Boston: Printed by J. Franklin, for N. Buttolph, B. / Eliot, and D. Henchman, and Sold at their Shops. 1721. Pages, (12), 288. 16 cm.

6. The / Office, Duty and Authority / of / Sheriffs, / How and in what Manner to execute the same, / according to the Common and Statute Laws / of Great-Britain, which are now in Force / and Use / Like wise, / Of Under-Sheriffs and their Deputies; / and where the High-Sheriff shall be answerable for / their Defaults, and where not, &c. / Together with the / Office and Duty of Coroners / Philadelphia: / Printed and Sold by Andrew Bradford, at the Bible / in the Second Street, MDCCXXI. *In* Conductor Generalis, 1722, no. 7, at page (233).

1722

7. Conductor Generalis, or / The Office, Duty and Authority / of / Justices of the Peace, / High Sheriffs, Under-Sheriffs, Goalers [*sic*], Coroners, / Constables, Jury Men, Over-seers of the Poor, / and also / The Office of Clerks of Assize / And of the Peace, &c. / Collected out of all the Books hitherto written on those / Subjects, whether of Common or Statute-Law. / To which is Added, / A Collection out of Sir Matthew Hales concerning / The Descent of Lands. / The whole Alphabetically digested under the several Titles, / With a Table directing to the ready finding out the proper / Matter under those Titles. / Printed and Sold by Andrew Bradford in Philadelphia, 1722. Pages, (8), 232, (2), 299, (1). 18 cm.

1727

8. The Constables Pocket-Book: / or, a / Dialogue / Between an / Old Constable & a New. / Being a Guide / In their Keeping the Peace, &c. / In Serving all Warrants. / Observing Orders of Courts. / Summoning Town Officers, and / Town-Meetings. / Collecting Rates and Assessments. / Serving Writs, Summons, & Executions / How to make

Returns of all Writs / and Warrants. / Form of Bail-Bonds &c. / An Account of all Lawful Fees. / The Second Edition, Corrected. / By N[icholas]. B[oone]. sometime since one of the Constables / for the Town of Boston, N. E. / Boston, Printed for and are to be Sold at the / Bible in Cornhill, 1727. Pages, 68. 15 cm. Mass. Hist. Soc.

1728

9. The / Right / of the / Inhabitants of Maryland, / to the / Benefit of the English Laws. / Oh Liberty! Oh Servitude! How amiable, how detestable are / the different Sounds! Liberty is Salvation in Politics, as Slavery / is Reprobation; nor is there any other Distinction, but that of Saint / and Devil, between the Champions of the one, and of the other. / Cato. / (*ornament.*) / Annapolis: Printed by W. Parks. MDCCXXVIII. Pages, (2), 3–4, 31. 17½ cm. Md. Hist. Soc.

1736

10. The / Office and Authority / of a / Justice of Peace. / And also / The Duty of Sheriffs, Coroners, Church- / wardens, Surveiors of Highways, Con- / stables, and Officers of Militia. / Together with / Precedents of Warrants, Judgments, Execu- / tions, and other legal Process, issuable by / Magistrates within their respective Jurisdic- / tions, in Cases Civil or Criminal. / And / The Method of Judicial Proceedings, before / Justices of Peace, in matters within their Cognisance / out of Sessions. / Collected from the Common and Statute Laws / of England, and Acts of Assembly, now in force; And / adapted to the Constitution and Practice of Virginia. / By George Webb, Gent. One of His Majesty's / Justices of Peace of the County of New-Kent. / Williamsburg: / Printed by William Parks. MDCCXXXVI. Pages, (2), iii–x, 364; Table (4). 20 cm.

1737

11. Remarks on Zenger's Tryal, taken out of the Barbados Gazette's for the benefit of the students in law, and others

in North America. Philadelphia: Printed by Andrew Bradford, 1737. pp. 71. 12mo. Evans, 4118. This, and the two following, are attributed by Evans to Jonathan Blenman.

12. The same. New York: Printed by William Bradford, 1737. Evans, 4119.

13. The same. Second edition. New-York: Printed by William Bradford, 1737. Evans, 4120. The London edition of 1738 states that the "Remarks were written by two eminent lawyers in one of our Colonies in America immediately after the publication of the Trial of Mr. Zenger."

1747

14. The Nature and Importance of Oaths and Juries, beautifully illustrated, and clearly explain'd, in Three Letters Extracted from a Number of political Pieces, and recommended as very necessary and useful to be perused and known by all members of Civil Government. By A Friend. To curb the Guilty, and the Just to spare, Has ever been, and still shall be our Care. New York. Printed and sold by Ja. Parker, at the New Printing-Office in Beaver-Street, 1747. 24 p. 16½ cm. N. Y. Public Library.

1749

15. Conductor Generalis: / or, the / Office, Duty and Authority / of / Justices of the Peace, / High-Sheriffs, Under-Sheriffs, Goalers [*sic*], Coroners, / Constables, Jury-men, and Overseers of the Poor. / As also / The Office of Clerks of Assize, / And of the Peace, &c. / Collected out of all the Books hitherto written on those Subjects, / whether of Common or Statute-Law. / The whole Alphabetically digested under the several Titles; with a / Table directing to the ready finding out the proper matter under / those Titles. / To which is added, / A Collection out of Sir Mathew Hales, concerning The Descent of / Lands; with several choice Maxims in Law, and the Office / of Mayors, &c. / The Second Edi-

tion, with large Additions. / Philadelphia: / Printed and Sold by B. Franklin, and D. Hall, at the New- / Printing-Office, near the Market, 1749. Pages, (16), xvi, 464. 18 cm.

16. Conductor Generalis / - - / - - - / - - - / - - - / - - - / - - - / - - - / - - - / - - - / - - - / - - - / - - / - - / - - - / - - - / - - - / - - - / - - - / The Second Edition, with large Additions. / New York: Printed and Sold by J. Parker, at the New-Printing-Office, / in Beaver-Street. 1749. Pagination identical with preceding. N. Y. State Library.

1750

17. Conductor Generalis / - - / - - - / - - / - - / - - / - - / - - / - - / - - / - - / - - / - - / - - / - - / - - / - - / - - / - - / The Second Edition, with large Additions. / Philadelphia: / Printed and sold by B. Franklin, and D. Hall, at the New- / Printing-Office, near Market. 1750. Pagination identical with two preceding items. 18 cm.

1751

18. The / Art / of / Pleading, / In Imitation of Part of / Horace's / Art of Poetry. / (*crown*) / New-York: / Printed and Sold by James Parker, at the New / Printing-Office, in Beaver-Street, 1751. Pages, (2), iii–vi, (1), 8–16. 18 cm. Not a legal treatise, but an interesting lampoon on lawyers and legal procedure. Probably by George Smalridge. See Evans, 6785, where the title appears to be incorrectly given.

1761

19. Des / Landmanns Advocat. / Das ist: / Kurzer Auszug / aus solchen / Gesetzen von Pennsylvania und England, / welche daselbst in völliger Kraft, und einem freyen Einwohner / auf dem Lande höchst nöthig und nützlich zu wissen sind. / Enthaltend / Anweisungen, / Welchergestalt der Landmann als ein Geschworner bey / Verhören und Rechtsprüchen, oder *Juryman*; als ein / Testamentsvollzieher, oder *Executor*; als ein Vormund, / oder *Guardian*; als ein Friedenhalter, oder *Constable*; / als ein Armen-pfleger, oder *Overseer of the Poor*, / u.s.w. sich zu betragen hat. / Nebst viel andern Dingen, durch deren Wissenschaft der gemeine Mann seinen / Schaden verhüten und seinen Nutzen beforderen kan. / Aus den Acten der Landsversammlung, oder *Acts of / Assembly*, und andern bewährtesten Englischen Büchern / zusammen getragen / von einem / Rechtsgelehrten: Und zum Besten der hiesigen Deutschen, in ihre Mutterspache übersetzt. / Philadelphia, Gedruckt bey Henrich Miller, in der Zwey- / ten-strasse, für den Verfasser. 1761. Pages, (5), ii–viii, 80; folding table; 81–122; folding table; 123–170; (3) register; (1) inlaid, Der gütige Leser beliebe etliche hier folgende fehler, so sich / in die Uebersetzung eingeschlichen, also zu verbessern: / 19½ cm.

Zuschrift, which follows the title page, is signed by David Henderson. The title page is printed in Gothic characters with the exception of those words italicized, which are in Roman.

20. The practical / Justice of the peace / and / Parish-officer, / of his Majesty's Province of / South-Carolina. / By William Simpson / One of the Assistant-Judges of the Court of General Sessions of / the Peace, Assize, &c. of the said Province. / Charlestown: / Printed by Robert Wells, opposite to the Exchange. / MDCCLXI. Pages, (4), v–viii, 276. 24 cm.

1764

21. Conductor Generalis: / or, the / Office, Duty and Authority / of / Justices of the Peace, / High-Sheriffs, Under-Sheriffs, Coroners, Constables, / Gaolers, Jury-Men, and Overseers of the Poor. / As also / The Office of Clerks of Assize, / And of the Peace, &c. / Compiled chiefly from Burn's Justice, and the several other books / on those Subjects, as far as they extend and can be adapted to these American Colonies. / By James Parker, One of his Majesty's Justices of the Peace for Middlesex County, in New-Jersey. /

The whole Alphabetically digested under the several Titles; with a Table / directing to the ready finding out the proper Matter under those Titles. / To which is added, / A Treatise on the Law of Descents in Fee-Simple: By William Blackstone, Esq; Barrister at Law, Vinerian Professor of the / Laws of England: With several choice Maxims in Law, &c. / Woodbridge, in New-Jersey: / Printed and Sold by James Parker: Sold also by David Hall, / Printer in Philadelphia. / M.DCC.LXIV. Pages, (3), iv–xvi, 592. 19 cm.

22. Another edition, otherwise identical with the above, has a title page containing the following: Sold also by John Holt, Printer in New York.

23. Another edition, otherwise identical, has a title page containing the following: Printed for, and sold by Garret Noel, near the Merchants Coffee House in New York. MDCCLXIV. Evans, 9775.

1766

24. Traité / des delits / et des peines, / traduit de l'Italien, / D'apres la troisieme Edition revue, cor- / rigée & augmentée par l'Auteur. / Avec des Additions de l'Auteur qui / n'ont pas encore paru en Italien. / Nouvelle Édition plus correcte / que les précédentes. / (*ornament.*) A Philadelphie. / M.DCC.LXVI. / Pages, xxxvj, 239. 16 cm. See Opere di Cesare Beccaria, Milan, 1821, vol. primo, pp. xxxiii, lxxv. This work, which is there stated to be the first edition of the French translation by the Abbé Morellet, was printed at Paris.

1767

25. The Conductor Generalis: or, the office, duty and authority of justices of the peace, high-sheriffs, under sheriffs, coroners, constables, gaolers, jury-men, and over-seers of the poor. As also, the office of Clerks of assize, and of the peace, &c. Compiled chiefly from Burn's Justice, and the several books on those subjects, as far as they extend and can be adapted to these American Colonies. By James Parker, esq. To which is added, A Treatise on the law of descents in fee-simple. By William Blackstone, esq; barrister at law, Vinerian professor of the Laws of England, New York: Printed and sold by James Parker, at the New Printing Office in Beaver-street, and David Hall in Philadelphia, 1767. Evans, 10721.

1768

26. The / County and Town Officer: / or an / Abridgment / of the / Laws / of the / Province of the Massachusetts-Bay, / Relative to / County and Town Officers. / By a Gentleman. / Good Laws are the best Support of Government. / Boston: / Printed by T. and J. Fleet, and Sold at the / Book-Store in Union-Street, 1768. Pages, (2), ii, 149; (3), a list of books which may be had, "At the Book-Store in Union-Street." 20 cm.

27. Every Man / His own Lawyer: / or, A Summary of the Laws of England, in a New / and Instructive Method, under the following / Heads, / Viz. / (*in double columns*) 1. Of Actions and Remedies, Writs, / Process, Arrests, and Bail. / II. Of Courts, Attornies and Solicitors / therein, Juries, Witnesses, Trials, / Executions, &c. / III. Of Estates and Property in Lands / and Goods, and how acquired; An- / cestors, Heirs, Executors and Ad- / ministrators. / IV. Of the Laws relating to Marriage, / Bastardy, Infants, Ideots, Lunaticks. / V. Of the Liberty of the Subject, Mag- / na Charta, the Habeas Corpus Acts / and other Statutes. / VI. Of the King and his Prerogative, / the Queen and Prince, Peers, Judges, Sheriffs, Coroners, Justices of Peace, / Constables, &c. / VII. Of publick Offences, Treason, / Murder, Felony, Burglary, Robbery, / Rape, Sodomy, Forgery, Perjury, &c. / And their Punishment. / (*end of double columns*) All of them so plainly treated of, that All Manner / of Persons may be particularly acquainted with our Laws and / Statutes, concerning Civil and Criminal Affairs, and know / how to defend Themselves and their Estates and Fortunes, / In all

Cases whatsoever. / The Seventh Edition, corrected and improved, with many / Additions, from Lord Raymond, Comyn, Strange, Foster, and / with the Statute Law down to 4 Geo 3. Inclusive. / New-York: / Printed by Hugh Gaine, Printer, Bookseller and / Stationer, at the Bible and Crown, in Hanover-Square, / M,DCC,LXVIII. Pages, (2), iii–iv, 289, table (9), index (3). 18 cm. By Giles Jacob.

1769

28. Every man his own lawyer. Philadelphia. John Dunlap, 1769. Hildeburn, 2438.

29. A / Treatise / on / Courts Martial, / Containing / (*double columns*) 1. Remarks on Martial / Law, and Courts Mar- / tial in general. / II. The Manner of Pro- / ceeding against Of- / fenders. / To which is added, / An Essay, / on Military Punishments and Rewards. / By Stephen Payne Adye / First Lieut. in the Royal Regiment of Artillery. / New-York: / Printed by H. Gaine, at the Bible and Crown, in / Hanover-Square, 1769. Pages, 1 p. l., ii, iv, 139 (1) p., 4 l. 18 cm. N. Y. Public Library.

1771

30. The Young Clerk's Vade Mecum, or complete English law tutor. The seventh edition. Philadelphia: Printed by W. and T. Bradford, 1771. Evans, 12296.

31. Commentaries / on the / Laws / of England / in four books. / By / Sir William Blackstone, Knt. / One of his Majesty's judges of the Court of Common Pleas. / Reprinted from the British Copy, / Page for Page with the Last Edition. / America: / Printed for the Subscribers, / By Robert Bell, at the late Union Library, in Third-street, / Philadelphia. MDCCLXXI. Second title page: Commentaries / on the / Laws / of / England. / Book the first. / Pages, (4), advertisements, (4), (1), ii, (6), (3), 4–485. 24 cm.

- - / - - / - - / - - / - - / Book the Second. / By / Sir William Blackstone, Knt. / - - - / - - - / - - - / America: / Printed for the Subscribers, / By Robert Bell, at the late Union Library, in Third-street. / Philadelphia. MDCCLXXI. Pages, (8), 520, xix. 24 cm.

1772

32. - - - / - - - / - - - / - - - / - - - / Book the Third. / By Sir William Blackstone, Knt. / - - - / - - - / - - - / America: / Printed for the Subscribers, / By Robert Bell, at the late Union Library, in Third-street, / Philadelphia. MDCCL-XXII. Pages, (8), 455, (1), xxvii. 24 cm.

- - - / - - - / - - - / - - - / - - - / Book the fourth. / By Sir William Blackstone, Knt. / - - - / - - - / - - - / America: / Printed for the Subscribers, / By Robert Bell, at the late Union Library, in Third-street, / Philadelphia [M]DCCL-XXII. Pages, (22), names of the subscribers; (8), 436, vii, (3), index. 24 cm.

33. An interesting / Appendix / to / Sir William Blackstone's Commentaries / on the / Laws of England. / Containing, / (*in double columns*) I. Priestley's Remarks on some / Paragraphs in the Fourth volume / of Blackstone's Commentaries, / relating to the Dissenters. / II. Blackstone's Reply to / Priestley's Remarks. / III. Priestley's Answer to / Blackstone's Reply. / IV. The Case of the late Election / of the County of Middlesex consi / dered on the Principles of the Con- / stitution and the Authorities of / Law. / V. Furneaux's Letters to the Hon. Mr. Justice Blackstone / concerning his Exposition of the / Act of Toleration, and some Posi- / tions relative to Religious Liberty, / in his celebrated Commentaries on / the Laws of England. / VI. Authentic copies of the Ar- / gument of the late Hon. Mr. Jus- / tice Foster in the Court of Jud- / ges Delegates, and of the Speech / of the Right Hon. Lord Mans- / field in the House of Lords, in / the Cause between the City of London and the Dissenters. / America: / Printed for the Subscribers, / By Robert

Bell, at the late Union-Library, in Third-street, / Philadelphia. MDCCLXXII.

Second title page: Remarks / on / some Paragraphs / In the Fourth Volume of / Dr. Blackstone's Commentaries on the / Laws of England, / relating to / The Dissenters. / By Joseph Priestley, LL.D.F.R.S. / (*two lines from*) Juvenal. / America: / Printed for the Subscribers, / By Robert Bell, at the late Union Library, in Third-street, / Philadelphia. MDCCLXXII.

Third title page: A / Reply / to / Dr. Priestley's / Remarks / on the/ fourth volume / of the / Commentaries / on the / Laws of England. / By the / Author of the Commentaries. / America: / Printed for the Subscribers. / By Robert Bell, at the late Union Library, in Third-street, / Philadelphia. MDCCLXXII.

Fourth title page: An / Answer / to / Dr. Blackstone's / Reply / to / Remarks / on the / fourth volume / of the / Commentaries / on the / Laws of England. / By Joseph Priestley, LL.D.F.R.S. / America: / Printed for the Subscribers, / By Robert Bell, at the late Union Library, in Third-street, / Philadelphia. MDCCLXXII.

Fifth title page: The / Case / of the / Late Election / for the County of Middlesex, / considered / On the Principles of the Constitition, / and the Authorities of Law. / [By Jeremiah Dyson.] America: / Printed for the Subscribers, / By Robert Bell, at the late Union Library, in Third-street, / Philadelphia. MDCCLXXII. Pages, (4), iv, 34, (3), 38–47, (4), 52–56, (3), 60–119. 24 cm.

34. (*Half title*) The / Englishman's Right; / A / Dialogue. / *verso*: As Jurymen are / liable to Doubts / in the Discharge / of their Duty, / This Treatise is / earnestly recom-/ mended, as giv- / ing their full In- / struction in every / Part of it. / (*Title page*) The / Englishman's Right; / A / Dialogue / between a / Barrister at Law / and a / Juryman; / Plainly setting forth, / I. The Antiquity, / II. The Excellent Designed Use, / III. The Office, and Just Privileges, / of Juries, / By the Law of England. / By Sir John Hawles,

Knight, / Solicitor-General to the late King William. / London, Printed M,DCC,LXXI. / Boston, / Re-printed by Edes and Gill, in Queen-Street, / M,DCC,LXXII. / Pages, (4), v–vii, 8–56. 16½ cm. Boston Athenaeum.

35. The Englishman's Right: A Dialogue between a Barrister at law, and a Juryman; setting forth the Antiquity, Use, Office, and just Privileges of Juries, by the Law of England. 1772. Hildeburn, 2782, from advertisement in Pennsylvania Chronicle, Mar. 9, 1772. This advertisement may refer, however, to the Boston edition, above, though Hildeburn speaks of a New York edition, which, however, has not been found.

36. The / Law / of / Crimes and Misdemeanors. / With the means of their Prevention and Punishment. / Exhibiting, / The Pleas of the State against the Offenders of Society, / Under the following heads: / I. The general nature of Crimes and Punishments. / II. The Persons capable of committing Crimes. / III. Their several degrees of Guilt as Principals or Accessories. / IV. The several species of Crimes, with the punishment annexed to each / by the Law. / V. The means of preventing the perpetration of Crimes. / VI. The Method of inflicting those Punishments which the Law has / annexed to each several Crime and Misdemeanor. / Containing a valuable Code of Criminal Law; Being / the Complete Book of the Celebrated Judge / Blackstone's Commentaries on Public Wrongs. / Philadelphia: / Printed and Sold by Robert Bell, in Third-street. / MDCCLXXII. 8vo. Hildeburn, 2751. The same as volume 4 of Blackstone's Commentaries, 1771–72, with added title page and list of subscribers omitted.

1773

37. Sixth title page to 1772 edition of Appendix to Blackstone's Commentaries: Letters / To the Honourable / Mr. Justice Blackstone, / concerning / His Exposition of the Act of Toleration, / and / Some Positions relative to Religious Liberty, / in his celebrated / Commentaries on the Laws of

England. / By Philip Furneaux, D.D. / The Second Edition with Additions, / and / An Appendix, containing Authentic Copies of the Argument / of the late Honourable Mr. Justice Foster in the Court of Judges De- / legates, and of the Speech of the Right Honourable Lord Mansfield / in the House of Lords, in the Cause between the City of London / and the Dissenters. / America: / Printed for the Subscribers, / By Robert Bell, at the late Union Library, in Third-street, / Philadelphia. MDCCLXXIII. Pages, xii, 155. 24 cm.

38. An interesting / Appendix / to / Sir William Blackstone's Commentaries / on the / Laws of England. / Containing, / (*double columns, as in* 1772 *edition.*) America: / Printed for the Subscribers, / By Robert Bell, at the late Union Library, in Third-street, / Philadelphia. MDCCL-XXIII. The second title page differs from the second title page, above, in the addition of two lines: Who can behold religious liberty curtailed, etc. Anon. The date on each of the title pages is MDCCLXXIII. Otherwise all of the title pages are identical with those in the previous edition. The paginations are, also, the same.

39. The / Palladium of Conscience; / or, the / Foundations of Religious Liberty displayed, asserted, and / established, agreeable to its true and genuine principles, above the reach / of all petty Tyrants, who attempt to lord it over the Human Mind. / Containing / Furneaux's Letters to Blackstone. / Priestley's Remarks on Blackstone. / Blackstone's Reply to Priestley. / And / Blackstone's Case of the Middlesex-Election; / With some other curious Tracts, worthy of high Rank in every / Gentleman's Literary Repository, / Being a necessary Companion for every Lover of / Religious Liberty. / And / An Interesting Appendix / to / Blackstone's Commentaries / on the / Laws of England. / America: / Printed for the Subscribers, / By Robert Bell, at the late Union Library, in Third-street, / Philadelphia, MDCCL-XXIII. Except for the title page, this edition is identical with the preceding.

40. The/ Security / of / Englishmen's Lives, / or the / Trust, Power and Duty / of the / Grand Juries / of / England, / Explained, according to the Fundamentals of the / English Governments, and the Declarations of / the same, made in Parliament by many Statutes. / The Fourth Edition. / Published for the Prevention of Popish Designs against the / Lives of many Protestant Lords and Commoners, who / stand firm to the Religion and ancient Government of / England. / London, Printed: / New-York: Re-printed by Hodge and Shober, / for Noel and Hazard. / M.DCC.-LXXIII. Pages, 101; (3), containing "Books / and / Stationary, / sold by Noel and Hazard." Library of Congress.

41. An / Abridgment / of / Burn's Justice of the Peace / and / Parish Officer. / To which is Added, / an / Appendix, / containing / Some general rules and directions necessary to be known and ob- / served by all justices of the peace. / Boston: / Printed for, and sold by Joseph Greenleaf, at his Printing-Office, / in Hanover-Street, near Concert Hall./ M,dcc,lxxiii. Pages, (5), 1 l. blank, 386, (2), advertisements. 22 cm.

1774

42. The / Young Clerk's / Magazine: / or, / English Law-Repository: / containing, / A Variety of the most useful Precedents / of Articles of Agreement, Bonds, Bills, Re- / cognizances, Releases, Letters and Warrants / of Attorney, Awards, Bills of Sale, Gifts, / Grants, Leases, Assignments, Mortgages, Sur- / renders, Jointures, Covenants, Copartner- / ships, Charterparties, Letters of Licence, Com- / positions, Conveyances, Partitions, Wills, and / all other Instruments that relate to Publick / Business. / With / Necessary Directions for making Distresses for Rent, / &c as the Law between Landlord and Tenant / now stands. / To which is added, / The Doctrine of Fines and Recoveries, and their / Forms. / Together with / Those of Common Writs, Affidavits, Memorials for / registering Deeds, &c in Middlesex; as also a / choice collection of Declarations in the King's Bench and Common Pleas. / The Fifth Edition, revised and corrected. / London Printed: / Philadelphia: / Reprinted by John Dunlap and Joseph Crukshank, / in Market-Street. / M.DCC.LXXIV. Pages, (4), 303. 16 cm.

43. The / Deputy Commissary's / Guide / Within the Province / of / Maryland / together / With plain and sufficient directions for Testators to form, and Executors / to perform their Wills and Testaments; for administrators to / compleat their Administrations, and for every Person any / way concerned in deceased Person's Estates, to proceed therein / with Safety to themselves and others. / (*figure of lion and anchor, with motto,* J'Espere.) by Elie Vallette. / Register of the Prerogative Office of the Said Province. / Annapolis, / Printed by Ann Catharine Green and Son. / MDCCLXXIV. T. Sparrow Sculp[t]. Pages, (2), (2), iii–iv, 248, (11), index. 20 cm. Unnumbered copper plate Table of Descents between pages 102 and 103. Title page engraved.

44. The / Office and Authority / of a / Justice of Peace / Explained and Digested, / Under proper Titles. / To which are added, / Full and correct Precedents of all Kinds of Process / necessary to be used by Magistrates; in which also the Duty of / Sheriffs, and other publick Officers, is properly discussed. / By Richard Starke, Esquire. / Williamsburg: / Printed by Alexander Purdie and John Dixon. / M,DCC,-LXXIV. Pages, (4), 356. 20½ cm. *Running title*: The Virginia Justice.

45. The Palladium of Conscience; or, the foundation of religious liberty displayed, asserted, and established. . . . And An Interesting Appendix to Blackstone's Commentaries on the laws of England. America: Printed for the Subscribers, by Robert Bell, at the late Union Library, in Third-street, Philadelphia, MDCCLXXIV. Evans, 13154, says that this is the third edition of An Interesting Appendix to Blackstone's Commentaries with a new general title. The special titles are all dated 1773. Pages 97–119 of The Case of the Late Election, and the title page, prefaces, and pages

1–4 of Furneaux's Letters (signatures N to R), were reprinted for this edition which otherwise is the same as the second edition.

46. English Liberties, / or the / Free-born Subject's Inheritance. / Containing / Magna Charta, Charta de Foresta, the Statute De Tal- / lagio non concedendo, the Habeas Corpus Act, and / several other Statutes; with Comments on each of / them. / Likewise, / Of Ship-Money: Of Tonnage and Poundage: Of Parliaments, and / the Qualification and Choice of Members: Of the Three Estates, / and of the Settlement of the Crown by Parliament. / Together with / A short History of the Succession, not by any hereditary Right: / Also a Declaration of the Liberties of the Subject: And of the / Oath of Allegiance and Supremacy. The Petition of Right: / with a short but impartial Relation of the Difference between / King Charles I. and the Long Parliament, concerning the / Prerogative of the King, the Liberties of the Subject, and the / Rise of the Civil Wars. Of Trials by Juries, and of the Qualifi- / cations of Jurors; their Punishment for Misbehaviour, and of / Challenges to them. / Lastly, / Of Justices of the Peace, and Coroners: With many Law-Cases / throughout the Whole. / Compiled first by Henry Care, and con- / tinued, with large Additions, by William / Nelson, of the Middle-Temple, Esq; / The sixth Edition, corrected and improved. / Providence, Rhode-Island; Printed and Sold by John Carter, at Shakespear's Head, in Meeting-Street, near the Court- / House. MDCC-LXXIV. Pages, (4), v–viii, 350, (6), names of subscribers. 17 cm.

47. The / Office and Authority / of a / Justice of Peace. / And also, / The Duty of Sheriffs, Coroners, Con- / stables, / Churchwardens, Overseers / of Roads, and other Officers. / Together with / Precedents of Warrants, Judgments, Execu-/ tions, and other legal Process, issuable by Ma- / gistrates within their several Jurisdictions, in Cases / Civil and Criminal, with the Method of Judicial / Proceedings before Justices of the Peace out of Sessi- / ons. / Also some Directions for their Conduct within / their County Courts. / To which is added, / An Appendix. / Containing many useful Precedents, and Directions / for the Execution of them. / Collected from the Common and Statute Laws of / England, and the Acts of Assembly of this Province, / and adapted to our Constitution and Practice. / By J. Davis, Esq; one of his Majesty's Justices of / the Peace for the County of Craven. / Newbern: Printed by James Davis. M,DCC,–LXXIV. Pages, (4), 404, (3), index. 20 cm. Ornamental border around title page.

48. Beccari. Dei delitti e delle pene. Philadelphie. Iohn Robert. Opere de Cesare Beccaria. Milan. 1821. Vol. primo. p. lxxvi.

1776

49. The Young Clerk's Vade Mecum: Or, Complete Law Tutor. Philadelphia: Robert Bell. 1776. Hildeburn, 3498.

50. The Young Clerk's / Vade Mecum: / or, / Compleat Law-Tutor. / Being a useful Collection of a great Variety / of the most approved Precedents in the Law, / and adapted to almost every Transaction in / Life wherein an Attention to legal Forms is / indispensably necessary. / And consisting chiefly of / (*double columns*) Bonds, / Special Conditions, / Letters of Attorney, / Awards, / Articles of Agree- / ment, / Bills of Sale, / Contracts, / Covenants, / Charter Parties, / Leases, / Proceedings upon Dis- / tress for Rent, / Assignments, / Deeds, / Indentures, / Mortgages, / Marriage Articles, / Wills, / Fines and Recoveries, / Writs, / Declarations and Pro- / ceedings at Law. / To which is added, / A Collection of English Precedents, / Relating to the / Office of a Justice of Peace. / Belfast Printed: / New York, Reprinted by H. Gaine, / in Hanover-Square, M,DCC,LXXVI.

Second title page: A / Collection / of / English Precedents, / Relating to the / Office / of a / Justice of Peace, / Consisting of / (*double columns*) Informations, / Summonses, / Orders, / Examinations, / Warrants, / Recognizances, / Committals, and / Other Instruments. / In an

Alphabetical Order. / To which is prefixed, / Copy of the Commission of the Peace; / with some Observations thereon./ Belfast printed: / New York, Re-printed, by H. Gaine, in Hanover / Square. MDCCLXXVI. Pages, (11), 236; (2), iii–iv, 86, (6), contents, (4), advertisements. 16½ cm.

1777

51. An / Essay / on / Crimes / and / Punishments, / Translated from the Italian; / with a / Commentary, / Attributed to Mons. De Voltaire. / Translated from the French. / In rebus quibuscumque difficilioribus non expectandum, ut quis / simul, & serat, & metat, sed praeparatione opus est, ut per gradus / maturescant. Bacon. / State of South Carolina. / Printed and sold by David Bruce, at / his shop in Church-street, Charlestown. / MDCCLXXVII. Pages, (3), iv–xii, 155. 18½ cm.

1778

52. (*Half title*) An / Essay / on / Crimes / and / Punishments. / (*First title page.*) An / Essay / on / Crimes / and / Punishments. / Written by the / Marquis Beccaria, / of Milan. / With a / Commentary, / Attributed to Monsieur De Voltaire. / (*Three lines from*) Voltaire. / (*Two lines from*) Brooke. / Philadelphia: / Printed and Sold by R. Bell, next door to St. Paul's / Church, in Third-Street. / M.DCC.–LXXVIII. (*Second half title.*) Remarks / on the / Opinions of some of the most celebrated Writers / on / Crown Law, / respecting the due distinction between / Manslaughter and Murder: / Being an Attempt to shew, / (*double columns*) That the plea of sudden Anger / cannot remove the imputation / and guilt of Murder, when a / Mortal Wound is wilfully given / with a Weapon: / That the indulgence allowed by / the Courts to voluntary Man- / slaughter in Rencounters, and / in sudden Affrays and Duels, / is indiscriminate, and without / foundation in Law: / And that impunity in such cases / of voluntary Manslaughter is / one of the principal causes of / the Continuance and present in- / crease of the base and disgrace- / ful practice of Duelling. / To which are added, some thoughts / on the particular case of the / Gentlemen of the Army, when / involved in such disagreeable / private differences. / With a Preparatory Address to the Reader, concerning the / Depravity and Folly of modern Men of Honour, falsely so called: / including a short account of the Principles and Design of the / Work. / By Granville Sharp. / Philadelphia: / Printed and Sold by R. Bell, in Third-Street. / M.DCC.LXXVIII. Pages, (4), (5), 6–352, (4). 19 cm.

53. Traité / des délits / et des peines. / Traduit de l'Italien. / D'apres la quatrieme Edition revue, / corrigée & augmentée par l'Auteur. / Avec des additions de l'Auteur qui / n'ont pas encore paru en Italien. / Nouvelle Edition plus correcte / que les précédentes. / (*ornament.*) / A Philadelphie / M.DCC.LXXVIII. Pages, xxxiv, 203. 15½ cm. It is doubtful whether this is an American print. Types and ornaments seem to point to a European origin.

1779

54. A / Treatise / on / Courts-Martial. / Containing, / I. Remarks on Martial-Law, and / Courts-Martial, in general. / II. The Manner of Proceeding against / Offenders. / To which is added / An / Essay / on / Military / Punishments and Rewards. / By Stephen Payne Adye, / Captain in the Royal Regiment of Artillery, / and / Judge-Advocate of the British Army in America. / Philadelphia: / Printed and sold by R. Aitken, opposite the / Coffee-House, Front-Street. / MDCCLXXIX. / 4 p. (1) 14–136. 14½ cm. N. Y. Public Library.

1783

55. Rudiments / of / Law and Government, / Deduced from / The Law of Nature; / Particularly addressed to the People of South- / Carolina, / But composed on Principles Applicable to all / Mankind. / - - - dicere Verum / Quid vetat. Hor. / Charlestown: / Printed by John M'Iver, jun.

No. 35½, on / the bay, north side of the Exchange. / MDCC-LXXXIII. / Pages, (2), iii–ix, 15–56. 18 cm. Boston Athenaeum; John Carter Brown Library.

56. An / Essay / on / Canon and Feudal Law. / By John Adams, Esquire; / Ambassador Plenipotentiary, from the / United and Independent States of North America, / To their High Mightinesses the States General of the / United Provinces of Holland. / To which is Annexed, the Political Character of the said / John Adams, Esquire; / By an American. / Philadelphia: / Printed and Sold by Robert Bell, in Third-Street, / M,DCC,LXXXIII. Pages, (44)–62. Title page on verso of p. 43. 21½ cm. Library of Congress. *In* Observations / on the / Commerce / of the American States / with/ Europe and the West Indies, / Including the several Articles of / Import and Export. / Price half a dollar. / Philadelphia: / Printed and sold by Robert Bell, in Third-Street, / M,DCC,-LXXXIII.

1787

57. Conductor-Generalis; or, the Office Duty and Authority of Justices of the Peace, Sheriffs, Coroners, Constables: to which are added several choice Maxims at Law. 8vo. New York, 1787. [By James Parker.] Marvin, Leg. Bib.

58. The Young Clerks vade mecum; or, compleat law tutor. Being a useful collection of a great variety of approved precedents in the law, and adapted to almost every transaction in life where an attention to legal forms is necessary. To which is added a collection of English precedents relating to the office of justice of peace. New-York: Printed by Hugh Gaine. 1787. Evans, 20906.

1788

59. (*Half title*) Mr. Trumbull's / Appeal / to the Public, respecting / Divorce. / (*title page*) An / Appeal to the Public, / especially to the learned, / with respect to the / Unlawfulness / of / Divorces, / In all Cases, excepting those of /

Incontinency. / The Substance of the Argument was pleaded be- / fore the Consociation of the County of New- / Haven, December 9th, 1785. / To which an Appendix is subjoined, / exhibiting a general View of the / Laws and Customs of Connecticut, / and of their Deficiency respecting / the Point in Dispute. / By Benjamin Trumbull, A. M. / Pastor of the Church in North-Haven. / "What therefore God hath joined together, let not man put asunder." / Jesus Christ. / New-Haven: Printed by J. Meigs. / A.D. M.DCC.LXXX-VIII. Pages, (5), 6–38; (1), Appendix; 40–53; (1), errata. 19½ cm.

60. The / South-Carolina / Justice of Peace, / containing all the / duties, powers and authorities of that office, as regu- / lated by the laws now of force in this state, / and / Adapted to the Parish and County Magistrate. / To which is added, a great variety of / warrants, indictments and other precedents, inter- / spersed under their several heads, / and a / summary of several of the decisions which have been / had in the courts of this state. / Entered in the Secretary's Office of the State of South-Carolina, 11th October, / 1788, agreeable to the Act of Assembly in that Case made and provided, enti- / tled "An Act for the Encouragement of Arts and Sciences." Ratified the / 26th March, 1784. Peter Freneau, Secretary. / Philadelphia: / Printed by R. Aitken & Son, at Pope's Head in / Market Street. / M.DCC.LXXXVIII. Pages, viii, 510, (2). 20½ cm. By J. F. Grimké.

61. The / Young Clerk's / Magazine: / or, / English Law-Repository: / containing, / A Variety of the most useful Precedents / of Articles of Agreement, Bonds, Bills, Re- / cognizances, Releases, Letters and Warrants / of Attorney, Awards, Bills of Sale, Gifts, / Grants, Leases, Assignments, Mortgages, Sur- / renders, Jointures, Covenants, Copartner- / ships, Charterparties, Letters of Licence, Com- /positions, Conveyances, Partitions, Wills, and / all other Instruments that relate to Public / Business. / With / Necessary Directions for making Distresses for Rent, / &c. as the Law between Landlord and Tenant / now stands. / To which is added, / The Doctrine of Fines and Recoveries, and their Forms. / The Sixth Edition, revised and corrected. / Philadelphia: / Printed by Joseph Crukshank, in Market-street, be- / tween Second and Third-streets. / MDCCLXXXVIII. Pages, (4), 299, (6), advertisements of books. 16 cm.

62. Conductor Generalis: / or the / Office, Duty and Authority / of / Justices of the Peace, / High-sheriffs, Under-sheriffs, Coroners, Constables, / Goalers [*sic*], Jury-men, and Overseers of the Poor. / As also, / The Office of Clerks of Assize / And of the Peace, &c. / To which are added / Several Choice Maxims in Law, &c. / Compiled chiefly from Burn's Justice, and the Several other Books / on those Subjects. / By James Parker, Esquire, late Justice of the Peace in / Middlesex County, in New Jersey. / Adapted to these United States. / The whole Alphabetically digested under the several Titles; with a / Table directing to the ready finding out the proper Matter under / those / Titles. / New-York: / Printed by John Patterson, for Robert Hodge, / No. 237, Queen-Street. / M.DCC.LXXXVIII. Pages, xvi, 539. 20 cm.

63. The / Conductor Generalis: / Or, The / Office, Duty and Authority / Of / Justices of the Peace, / High-Sheriffs, Under-Sheriffs, Coroners, / Constables, Gaolers, Jury-Men, And / Overseers of the Poor. / As Also / The Office of Clerks of Assize, / And of the Peace, Etc. / Compiled chiefly from Burn's Justice, and the several other Books / on those subjects, by James Parker, late one of the Justices / of the Peace for Middlesex County, in New-Jersey; and now / revised and adapted to the United States of America. / By A Gentleman of the Law. / The whole Alphabetically digested under the several Titles; with a Table / directing to the ready finding out the proper matter under those Titles. / To which Are Added, / (Above what is in any other Edition of this Work,) / The Act called the Ten Pound Act, and the Militia Law / of the State of New-York. / New-York: / Printed by Hugh Gaine, and sold at his Book-Store at the Bible in / Hanover-Square, 1788. Pages, 461. N. Y. State Library.

64. An / Introduction / To The / Law / relative to / Trials at Nisi Prius / The Fifth Edition / With Additions and Corrections / By Francis Buller, Esq; / Of the Middle Temple. / London, Printed: / New-York: Reprinted by Hugh Gaine, at his Book-Store / and Printing-Office, at the Bible, in Hanover-Square. / M,DCC,LXXXVIII. Pages, (3), iv–v, (1), 2–336; index, (30); (1) advertisement. 21½ cm. N. Y. Public Library; John Carter Brown Library.

65. The / Law / of / Evidence / By the late Lord Chief Baron / Gilbert. / The Fifth Edition, corrected; / with / Many Additions; and a Compleat / Table to the Whole. / London, Printed: / Philadelphia: / Re-printed and Sold by Joseph Crukshank, / in Market-Street, between Second / and Third-Streets. / MDCCLXXXVIII. Pages, (4), 286, (75), table. 19½ cm.

1789

66. A / System / of the / Law / of / Marine Insurance, / with three chapters / on / Bottomry; on Insurances on Lives; / and on / Insurances against Fire. / By James Allan Park, Esq. / Of Lincoln's Inn, / Barrister at Law. / Lex (de qua agimus) est fons aequitatis. Cicero. / London: Printed. / Philadelphia: Re-printed / By Joseph Crukshank, in Market-Street, between Second / and Third-Streets. / M,DCC,LXXXIX. Pages, xvi, (8), xliv, 530, (45). 20 cm.

67. A / Treatise / on the / Pleadings / in / Suits / in the / Court of Chancery / by English bill. / In two books. / By John Mitford, Esq. / Philadelphia. / Printed by Rice and Co. Market-street. / M,DCC,LXXXIX. Pages, (7), viii–xv, 128. 17 cm.

1790

68. The Conductor generalis; or the office, duty and authority of justices of the peace, high sheriffs, under-sheriffs, coroners, constables, gaolers, jurymen, and overseers of the poor. As also, the office of clerks of assize, and of the peace, &c. Compiled chiefly from Burn's Justice; and the several other books on those subjects. By James Parker, esquire, late one of the justices of the peace for Middlesex County in New-Jersey; and now revised and adapted to the United States of America. By a Gentleman of the law. The whole alphabetically digested under the several titles; with a table, directing to the ready finding out the proper matter under those titles. To which are added (above what is in any other edition of the work) the Act called the Ten pound Act, and the Militia law of the State of New-York. New-York: Printed by Hugh Gaine, 1790. Evans, 22754.

69. Commentaries / on the / Laws / of / England. / In Four Books. / By / Sir William Blackstone, Knt. / One of the late Justices of his Britannick Majes- / ty's Court of Common Pleas. / In Four Volumes. / The First Worcester Edition, / Carefully reprinted from the last London Edition. / Containing, / The Last Corrections of the Author, / The additions by Richard Burn, LL.D. / And Continued to the Present Time, / By John Williams, Esq. / Vol. I — Book I. (Vol. II — Book II.); (Vol. III — Book III.); (Vol. IV — Book IV.) / Printed at Worcester, Massachusetts. / By Isaiah Thomas, / Sold at his bookstore in Worcester, and by him and / Company in Boston. / MDCCXC. Vol. I — Frontispiece portrait of Blackstone, engraved by S. Hill, vi, (7–9), 10–485. Vol. II—vii, 520, xix, folding table of descents opposite page 240. Vol. III—vi, 455, xxvii. Vol. IV—vi, 443, vii, (52), index. 17½ cm.

1791

70. A Full, clear, and familiar explanation of the law concerning bills of exchange, promissory notes, and the evidence on a trial by jury relative thereto, with a description of bank notes, and the privilege of attornies. By Peter Lovelass, of the Inner Temple, gent. author of the Law's disposal. The third edition. Philadelphia: Printed by Joseph Crukshank, no. 91, High-Street, between Second and Third-Streets. MDCCXCI. Pages, x, (135). 8vo. Evans, 23510, "Unpaged. The marginal reference, giving the pages of the Third English edition, of which it is a reprint."

71. The / Town Officer; / or the / Power and Duty of / (*double columns*) Selectmen, / Town Clerks, / Town Treasurers, / Overseers of the Poor, / Assessors, / Constables, / Collectors of Taxes, / Surveyors of High Ways, / Surveyors of Lumber, / Fence Viewers, / And other Town Officers. / As contained in the Laws of the Commonwealth of Massachusetts. / With a variety of Forms for the use of such Officers. / To which are added, / The Power and Duty of Towns, / Parishes and Plantations; / And a plain and regular Method to keep Accounts of the Expendi- / tures of Monies voted by a Town; upon an inspection of which, / the state of its Finances may at any time be known. / By Samuel Freeman, Esq. / [With the Priviledge of Copy Right.] / Portland: / Printed by Benjamin Titcomb, Jun. MDCCXCI. Pages, (5), 6–178, (2). 17 cm.

72. A / Digest / of the / Law of Actions / at / Nisi Prius. / In two volumes. / Vol. I. / By Isaac 'Espinasse, Esq. / Of Gray's Inn, Barrister at Law. / Et Spes et Ratio Studiorum- / Juv. / Philadelphia: / Printed by J. Crukshank, and W. Young, / Booksellers and Stationers. / M,DCC,XCI. Title page of volume two identical with above, except for substitution of Vol. II for Vol. I. Vol. 1. Pages, (24), 434, (46). 17 cm. Vol. 2. Pages, (3), iv–xviii, 518. 17 cm.

73. The / Office and Authority / of a / Justice of the Peace, / and of / Sheriffs, Coroners, &c. / According to the Laws / of the / State of North-Carolina. / By François-Xavier Martin, Esquire, / Attorney at Law. / Happy the Country where Law is not a Science! / Newbern: / François-Xavier Martin. / 1791. 19½ cm. Pages, (4), (3), (1), (5)–6, 307, (1), errata, (6), subscribers.

74. An / Introductory / Lecture / to a / Course of Law Lectures. / By James Wilson, L.L.D. / To which is added, / A Plan of the Lectures. / Philadelphia: / From the Press of T. Dobson. / M,DCC,XCI. Pages, (5), 6–96. 20 cm.

1792

75. The / Young Clerk's / Magazine: / or, / English Law-Repository: / containing, / a variety of the most useful Precedents / of Articles of Agreement, Bonds, Bills, Re- / cognizances, Releases, Letters and Warrants / of Attorney, Awards, Bills of Sale, Gifts, / Grants, Leases, Assignments, Mortgages, Sur- / renders, Jointures, Covenants, Copartner- / ships, Charterparties, Letters of Licence, Com- / positions, Conveyances, Partitions, Wills, and / all other Instruments that relate to Public / Business. / With / necessary Directions for making Distresses for Rent, / &c. as the Law between Landlord and Tenant / now stands. / To which is added, / The Doctrine of Fines, and Recoveries, and their / Forms. / The seventh Edition, revised and corrected. / Philadelphia: / Printed by Joseph Crukshank, No. 87, High-street, / MDCCXCII. Pages, (iv), 299, (6), containing advertisements headed: American Editions / of the following / Books / may be had of Joseph Crukshank. 17 cm. John Carter Brown Library.

76. Burn's / Abridgment, / or the / American Justice; / containing the whole / Practice, Authority and Duty / of / Justices of the Peace; / with correct forms of precedents / relating thereto, and adapted / to the present situation / of the / United States. / Dover, (New-hampshire.) / Printed for, and sold by Eliphalet Ladd, at / his printing-office, near the court-house. / M,DCC,XCII. / Pages, viii, 179, 190–269, 280–359, 370–484, (1). One preface, signed E. Ladd, Dover, February 29, 1792. 18 cm.

77. Burn's / Abridgment, / or the / American Justice; / containing the whole / Practice, Authority and Duty / of / Justices of the Peace; / with correct forms of precedents / relating thereto, and adapted / to the present situation / of the / United States. / The second Edition. / Dover, (New-hampshire.) / Printed for, and sold by Eliphalet Ladd, at / his printing-office, near the Court-house. / M,DCC,XCII. Pages, (5), vi-viii, 179, 190–269, 280–359, 370–484, (1).

18½ cm. Two prefaces, the first dated, Dover, February 29, 1792; the second, Dover, August 30th, 1792. An exact reprint of the first edition, with the exception of the second preface.

78. The / Conductor Generalis: / or, the / Office, Duty and Authority / of / Justices of the Peace, / high-sheriffs, under-sheriffs, coroners, / constables, gaolers, jury-men, and / overseers of the poor. / As also, / The Office of Clerks of Assize, / And of the Peace, &c. / Compiled chiefly from Burn's Justice, and the several other Books, / on those Subjects, by James Parker, late one of the Justices / of the Peace for Middlesex County, in New-Jersey; and now / revised and adapted to the United States of America. / By a gentleman of the law. / The whole Alphabetically digested under the several Titles; with a Table / directing to the ready finding out the proper Matter under those Titles. / To which are added, / The Excise and Militia Laws of the United States; and the / Acts called the Ten Pound Act of the States of / Pennsylvania and New-York. / Philadelphia: / Printed for Robert Campbell. / 1792. Pages, (5), vi–xv, 464. 21 cm.

79. The / Principles / of / Natural and Politic / Law, / in two volumes. / By J. J. Burlamaqui, / Counsellor of State, and late professor of natural and / civil law at Geneva. / Translated into English by Mr. Nugent. / The fourth edition, revised and corrected. / Boston: / Printed by Joseph Bumstead, for John Boyle, marl- / borough-street, Benjamin Larkin, cornhill, / and James White, court-street. / M.DCC.–XCII. Pages, (6), vii–viii, (20), 424. 20½ cm. Vol. 2 begins, page [193]. Half title followed immediately on same page by text, as follows: The / Principles / of / Politic Law; / being a sequel to the / Principles of the Law of Nature. / Vol. II.

1793

80. An / Essay / on / Crimes and Punishments: / by the / Marquis Beccaria, of Milan. / With a / Commentary, / by / M. de Voltaire. / A new edition corrected. / In rebus quibuscumque difficilioribus non expectandum, ut quis / simul, & serat, & metat, sed praeparatione opus est, ut per gradus maturescant. Bacon. / Philadelphia: / Printed by William Young, No. 52, Second- / street, the corner of Chestnut-street. / M,DCC,XCIII. Pages, (3), iv–x, (1), 14–160; (1), A / Commentary / on the book of / Crimes and Punishments. / *verso blank*; (1), 164–230. 15½ cm. American Antiquarian Society; John Carter Brown Library.

81. (*Half title.*) Chipman's / Principles of government. / (*Title page*) Sketches / of the / Principles of Government; / By Nathaniel Chipman / Judge of the Court of the United States, / for the District of Vermont. / Rutland: / From the Press of J. Lyon: / Printed for the Author: / June, M,DCC,-XCIII. Pages, (5), iv, (2), ix–xii, (1), 14–292. 16½ cm.

82. Reports / and / Dissertations, / in two parts. / Part I. / Reports of Cases determined in the Supreme / Court of the State of Vermont, in the / years 1789, 1790, and 1791. / Part II. / Dissertations on the Statute adopting the Com- / mon Law of England, the Statute of / Conveyances, the Statute of Off- / sets, and on the Negotiabil- / ity of Notes. / With an Appendix, containing / Forms of Special Pleadings in several cases; Forms of / Recognizances; of Justices Records; and of / Warrants of Commitment. / By Nathaniel Chipman, / late chief-justice. / Rutland: / Printed by Anthony Haswell, / for the author; M,DCC,XCIII.

Second title page: Part First. / Reports of Cases / determined in the / Supreme Court / of the / State of Vermont. /

Third title page: Part II. Dissertations / On the Statute adopting the / Common Law of England, / The / Statute of Conveyances, / The / Statute of Offsets, / And on the / Negotiability of Notes. Pages, (9), 10–110, 1 leaf blank, (5), 118–139, (2), 142–166, (1), 168–180, (1), 182–225, (2), 228–230, (1), 232–296. 15½ cm. Page 229 is misnumbered 129; page 233 is misnumbered 133; page 280 is misnumbered 082.

83. The Instructor generalis, or general instructor: for all town, parish and county officers. Containing the duty of each, with the laws of the State, as it applies to their several offices. By Jonathan Rawson, esq. Dover, New-Hampshire: Printed by Eliphalet Ladd, 1793. pp. 200? Evans, 26055. 9th New Hampshire District Copyright, issued to Jonathan Rawson, as Author, 27 May, 1793. No copy has been found and it may never have been printed.

84. The / Probate Auxiliary; / Or, a Director and Assistant to / Probate Courts, Executors, Admi- / nistrators and Guardians. / Being the laws of the commonwealth of / Massachusetts, respecting the estates / of Testators, Intestates and / Wards. / Carefully collected. / Together with a comprehensive alpha- / betical Index to the same. / To which are added, / a variety of Forms, for the use of pro- / bate courts, and of such persons as may have business to transact therein. / By Samuel Freeman, Esq. / Register of Probate for the County of Cumberland. / [With the Privelege of Copy Right.] / Portland: (Massachusetts) printed by / Benjamin Titcomb, jun. / 1793. Pages, (3), iv–xi, (1), 72, (3), 74–95, (2), 98–153, (1), 155–156. 17 cm.

85. The / Town Officer; / or the / Power and Duty of / (*double columns*) Selectmen, / Town Clerks, / Town Treasurers, / Overseers of the / Poor, / Assessors, / Constables, / Collectors of Taxes, / Surveyors of High / Ways, / Surveyors of Lumber, / Fence viewers, / And other Town Officers. / As contained in the / Laws of the Commonwealth of / Massachusetts. / With a Variety of Forms, / for the Use of such Officers. / To which are added, / The Power and Duty of / Towns, Parishes and Planta- / tions. / And a plain and regular Method to keep Ac- / counts of the Expenditures of Monies / voted by a Town; upon an inspection of which, / the state of its Finances may at any time be / known. / By Samuel Freeman, Esq. / Printed at Boston, / by I. Thomas and E. T. Andrews, / Proprietors of the Work. / Faust's Statue. No. 45 Newbury Street. / MDCCXCIII. Pages, (3), iv, (3), 8–239, (1), advertisements. 17½ cm.

86. The / Civil and Executive / Officer's Assistant. / Containing the forms of / (*double columns*) Bonds, / Bills, / Deeds, / Letters of Attorney, / Policies of Insurance, / Releases, / Wills, / Writs, / Pleas, / Officers returns / and Justices re- / cords of Court. / With the power and duty of / Justices of the Peace / as contained in the Laws of the State of / Connecticut / and exhibiting the Duty and Province of / Select-men, Constables, Grand-jurors, &c. / With an Appendix containing a concise mode of casting In- / terest, keeping town accompts, and transacting Public / Business with facility and accuracy. / By John Goodrich, Esq. / Printed and Sold by Abel Morse, / in State-Street New-Haven. / M,DCC,XCIII. Pages, (4), v–xii, 9–54, 54, 56–168, 167–224, 226, 225, 227–236, 235–238, 237–254, 253–305. 19 cm.

87. An / Enquiry / how far / the punishment of death is necessary / In Pennsylvania. / With / Notes and Illustrations. / By William Bradford, esq. / To which is added, / an account of the gaol and penitentiary house of / Philadelphia, and of the interior manage- / ment thereof. / By Caleb Lownes, of Philadelphia. / If we enquire into the cause of all human corruptions, we shall / find that they proceed from the impunity of crimes, and not from the / moderation of punishments. Montesq. / Philadelphia: / printed by T. Dobson at the Stone-house, No. 41, / South Second-Street, / M,DCC,XCIII.

Half title, after page 46: Notes / and / Illustrations.

Second title page, after page 72: An / Account / of the / Alteration And Present State / of the / Penal Laws / of / Pennsylvania, / containing also an account of the goal [*sic*] and / penitentiary house of Philadelphia and the / interior management thereof. / By / Caleb Lownes. Pages, (3); single page numbered 4; (1), 4–46; (1) half title, verso blank; (1); 50–72; *folding table*: A Table exhibiting a View of the number of Persons convicted of all Capital and certain other Crimes. / ; (1), second title page, verso blank; (1), 76–93; (1), Appendix /, verso blank; (1), 98–108. 20 cm.

1794

88. A / Treatise / On The / Practice / Of The / Supreme Court Of Judicature / Of The / State Of New-York / In / Civil Actions. / By William Wyche, / Of The Honorable Law Society Of Grey's Inn, London; / And Citizen Of The United States Of America. / Lex mundi harmonia. / (*ornament.*) / New-York: / Printed by T. and J. Swords, No. 167, William-Street. / –1794– Pages, xvi, 355, (1). 21 cm. N. Y. Public Library.

89. *Half title*: Practice / of the / Supreme Court / of the / State of New-York. / *Title page*: A / Treatise / on the / Practice / of the / Supreme Court of Judicature / of the / State of New-York / in Civil Actions. / The second edition. / By William Wyche, / of the honorable Law Society of Grey's Inn, London; / and citizen of the United States of America. / Lex mundi harmonia. / (*ornament.*) / New-York: / Printed by T. and J. Swords, No. 167, William-Street, / 1794. Pages, (7), viii–xvi, 355, (1), errata, (3), advertisements. 21 cm.

90. A Collection of Entries, or Select Pleadings, in the Supreme Court of Judicature of the State of New York. By William Wyche. [1794?] Proposals for publishing this, dated New York, May 1, 1794, are advertised on the second to the last page of the preceding.

91. The / Town Officer: / or the / Power and Duty of / (*double columns*) Selectmen, / Town Clerks, / Town Treasurers, / Overseers of the Poor, / Assessors, / Constables, / Collectors of Taxes, / Surveyors of Highways, / Surveyors of Lumber, / Fence Viewers, / Clerks of the Market, / Measurers of Wood, / And other Town Officers. / As contained in the / Laws of the Commonwealth of Massachusetts. / With a / Variety of Forms, / for the Use of such Officers. / To which are added, / The Power and Duty of / Towns, Parishes and Plantations, / and a / Plain and regular Method to Keep Accounts / of the Expenditures of Monies voted by a / Town; upon an Inspection of which, the State of its / Finances may at any Time be known. / The Third Edition. / Corrected, improved and greatly enlarged. / By Samuel Freeman, esq. / Author of the Probate Auxilliary, and American Clerk's Magazine. / Published According to Act of Congress. / Printed at Boston, / by I. Thomas and E. T. Andrews, / proprietors of the work. / Faust's Statue, no. 45, Newbury Street. / MDCCXCIV. Pages, (3), v, (4), 9–240. 17 cm.

92. The / New Vade Mecum; / Or, / Young Clerk's Magazine; / Digested and improved to correspond with the Laws / of the State of New-York in particular, / and the United States in general: / Containing / A variety of the most useful Precedents, adapted to / almost every Transaction in Life; / Such As / Articles of Agreement, Awards, Bonds, Conditions, Recogni- / zances, Letters and Warrants of Attorney, Covenants, Re- / leases, Indentures, Charter-Parties, Copartnerships, Bar- / gain, and Sales. Gifts, Grants, Exchanges, Leases, Mortga- / ges, Assignments, Defeasances, Surrenders, Uses, Trusts, / Conveyances by Lease and Release, Feoffments, Jointures, / marriage Settlements, Wills and Codicils, Levying of Fines, / &c. &c. &c. / — To Which Is Added — / A Collection of Forms of Writs, &c most common in / Use in the Supreme Court of the State of / New-York. / The First Edition. / — Entered According To Law — / Lansingburgh: / Printed by Silvester Tiffany, for, and sold by, Tho's / Spencer, at his Book Store, in Albany. / MDCCXCIV. Pages, (7), 8–288, 299–346. Page 93 is misnumbered 63; page 97, 79. 15½ cm. N. Y. Public Library has a copy of this with minor variations on the title page and other pages.

93. Precedents / in the / Office / of a / Justice of Peace. / To which is added / A Short System of Conveyancing, / in a method entirely new. / With an / Appendix, / containing a variety of the most useful forms. / By Collinson Read, Esquire. / Philadelphia, Printed by Hall and Sellers, No. 51, Market-Street, / M.DCC.XCIV.

Second title page: A / Short System / of / Conveyancing, / in a method entirely new. / (*Then follows a* Table, Explanation and Example.) Pages, (4), 39, (4), 44–63; 33, Appendix, (1), Table of Contents; (1), errata. 19½ cm.

94. The / Conductor Generalis: / or, the / Office, Duty and Authority / of / Justices of the Peace, / high-sheriffs, under-sheriffs, coroners, constables, / gaolers, jury-men, and overseers of the poor. / As also, / The Office of Clerks of Assize, / And of the Peace, &c / Compiled chiefly from Burn's Justice, and the several other/ Books, on those Subjects, by James Parker, late one of the / Justices of the Peace for Middlesex County, in New-Jer- / sey; and now revised and adapted to the United States / of America, / by a gentleman of the law. / The whole Alphabetically digested under the several Titles; with a / Table directing to the ready finding out the proper / Matter under those Titles. / Albany: / Printed by Charles R. & George Webster, / On the West Corner of State and Pearl-streets, near the / English Church, and opposite the City-Tavern, 1794: / And sold at their Office, and at the Book-Stores of Webster & Steel, Thomas Spencer / and Abraham Ellison, Albany; by Mr. Wands, Lansingburgh, and Mr. Stoddard, / Hudson; and, in the City of Philadelphia, at the Book-Stores of / Mr. Mathew Carey, and Mr. William Young. Pages, (4), v–xv, 17–467. 20 cm.

95. An introductory / Lecture / to a / Course of Law Lectures, / delivered November 17, 1794. / By James Kent, Esquire, / Professor of Law in Columbia College. / Published at the request of the trustees. / New-York: / Printed by Francis Childs. / 1794. Pages, (3), 4–23. 25½ cm.

96. An / Essay / on the / Theory and Practice / of / Fines; / with / Precedents. / By William Wyche, / of the Honorable Law Society of Grey's Inn, London; Author of / the Treatise on the Practice of the Supreme Court of New-York; / and Citizen of the United States of America. / Lex mundi harmonia. / (*device.*) / New-York: / Printed and sold by T. and J. Swords, No. 167, William-Street; / sold also by J. Rivington, No. 156, Pearl-Street. / — 1794 — Pages, 78, (1). 21½ cm. N. Y. Public Library.

97. Valuable Assistant to Every Man: / or, / American Clerk's Magazine. / Containing / All the Useful and Necessary / Forms of Writings, / which continually occur between Man and Man, under / the Names of / (*triple columns*) Acquittances, / Agreements, / Assignments, / Awards, or Arbi- / trations, / Bargains, / Bills of Sale, / Bonds, / Conditions, / Conveyances, / Covenants, / Deeds, / Feoffments, / Fines and Recov- / ery, / Gifts and Grants, / Indentures, / Interest Tables, / Leases, / Lease &c Release, / Letters of Attor- / ney, / Mortgages, / Notes, / Pleas, / Receipts, / Releases, / Sales, / Surrenders, / Wills and Testa- / ments, / Writs and De- / clarations, &c. / And other Instruments, / The Whole of which are calculated for the / Use of the Citizens of the United States, / And conformable to Law. / By Samuel Freeman, Esq; / Author of the Town Officer and Probate Auxiliary. / Published according to Act of Congress. / Printed at Boston, / By I. Thomas and E. T. Andrews. / Sold by them at Faust's Statue, No. 45, Newbury Street, and / by said Thomas in Worcester. / 1794. Pages, v, (3), 10–223, (1), with errata. 18 cm.

1794

98. An / Account / of the / Alteration and Present State / of the / Penal Laws / of / Pennsylvania, / containing also an account of the gaol / and penitentiary house of / Philadelphia / and the interior management thereof / By Caleb Lownes. / Lexington: / Printed by J. Bradford at the corner of / Main and Cross Streets / M,DCC,XCIV. Pages, (3), 4–20. 21 cm.

1795

99. A / Valuable Assistant to Every Man: / or, the / American Clerk's Magazine. / Containing the most Useful and Necessary / Forms of Writings, / Which commonly occur between Man and Man, under / the Names of / (*triple* *columns*) Acquittances, / Agreements, / Assignments, / Awards, / Bargains, / Bills of Sale, / Bonds, / Conditions, / Conveyances, / Covenants, / Deeds, / Feoffments, / Fine and Recov- / ery, / Gifts and Grants, / Indentures, / Leases, / Lease & Release, / Letters of Attor- / ney, / Mortgages, / Notes, / Pleas, / Receipts, / Releases, / Sales, / Surrenders, / Wills, Writs and Decla- / rations, &c. / And other Instruments, / The whole of which are calculated for the / Use of the Citizens of the United States. / And conformable to Law. / By Samuel Freeman, Esq: / Compiler of the Town Officer, / Probate Auxiliary, and / Massachusetts Justice. / The Second Edition, / Revised, Corrected and Considerably Enlarged. / Published according to Act of Congress. / Printed at Boston, / By I. Thomas and E. T. Andrews, / Sold by them at Faust's Statue, No. 45, Newbury Street, and / by said Thomas in Worcester. — Also, at the Bookstore / of Thomas, Andrews and Butler, Market / Street, Baltimore. — 1795. Pages, (3), single page numbered iv, (3), 8–247, (1), advertising works, "Lately published, compiled by the Author of this Work." 17 cm.

100. Laws and Usages / respecting / Bills Of Exchange, / and / Promissory Notes. / Compiled from the best authorities. / By John Tisdall, / notary public [*sic*] of Belfast, / With such alterations and additions as may / render this treatise more useful to / the citizens of Pennsylvania, by / W. F. esq. of Philadelphia. / Philadelphia: / Printed for T. Stephens, No. 60, south second- / street, by F. R. Bailey. / M,DCC,XCV. Pages, (3), single page numbered iv, 55. 19½ cm.

101. The / New Virginia Justice / comprising the / office and authority / of a / Justice of the Peace, / in the / Commonwealth of Virginia. / Together / With a variety of useful Precedents / adapted to the Laws now in force. / To which is added, / An Appendix containing all the most approved forms of / Conveyancing, commonly used in this country, / Such as Deeds, of Bargain and Sale, of / Lease and Release, of Trust, Mort- / gages, &c. — Also the duties of / a Justice of the Peace aris- / ing under the Laws of / the United States. / By William Waller Hening, / Attorney at Law. / Richmond; Printed by T. Nicolson, 1795. Pages, (19), containing list of subscribers; title page, verso blank; (15), 2–456; (11), index; xxiv, Appendix No. I / to the / New Virginia Justice, &c. / containing / Forms of conveyancing; / 32, Appendix No. II. / to the / New Virginia Justice, &c. / containing / The Duties of a Justice of the Peace / arising under the / Laws of the United States. 20 cm.

102. Dissertations: / being the / Preliminary Part / of / A Course Of Law Lectures. / By James Kent. / professor of law in Columbia College. / New-York: / Printed by George Forman, No. 156, Front-street, / For the Author. — 1795. Pages, (5), 6–87. 20 cm.

103. The / Young / Clerk's Magazine: / or, / English Law-Repository: / containing / A Variety of the most useful Precedents of / (*double columns*) Articles of Agreement, / Bonds, / Bills, / Recognizances, / Releases, / Letters and Warrants / of Attorney, / Awards, / Bills of Sale, / Gifts, / Grants, / Leases, / Assignments, / Mortgages, / Surrenders, / Jointures, / Covenants, / Copartnerships, / Letters of Licence, / Compositions, / Conveyances, / Partitions, / Wills, / and all other / Instruments that relate to Public Business. / With / Necessary Directions for making Distresses for Rent, &c. / as the Law between Landlord and Tenant now stands. / To which is added, / The Doctrine of Fines and Recoveries, / and their Forms. / The eighth edition, revised and corrected. / Philadelphia: / Printed for and sold by Joseph Crukshank, / no. 87, High-street, / 1795. Pages, (4), 299, (6), advertisement, American Editions / of the following / Books / may be had of / Joseph Crukshank. 16 cm.

104. Summary / of the / Law of Nations, / founded on / the Treaties and Customs / of the / Modern Nations / of / Europe, / with / a list of the principal treaties, / concluded since the year 1748 down to the present time, / indicating the works in which they are / to be found. / By Mr. Martens, / professor of law in the University of Gottingen. / Translated from the French / by William Cobbett. / Philadelphia: / published by Thomas Bradford, printer, / bookseller & stationer, / No. 8, South Front Street. / 1795. Pages, (3), iv–xix, (1), 375. The last nine pages contain a list of subscribers' names. 26 cm.

105. The / Massachusetts Justice: / being / A Collection of the Laws / of the / Commonwealth of Massachusetts, / Relative to the Power and Duty of / Justices of the Peace. / Alphabetically arranged, in Two Parts. / Part I. — The Power and Duty of the Justices of the / Court of General Sessions of the Peace, / Part II. — The Power and Duty of Justices of the Peace, in their Separate Capacity. / To which are added, under the proper Heads, / A Variety of Forms, / Grounded on said Laws. / The whole intended for the Use of those who Practise in the / Office of a Justice, to assist them in the various Duties / thereto belonging. / With an Appendix, / containing short and concise Rules for changing Pounds, Shillings, Pence / and Farthings, into Dollars, Cents and Milles, which a late Law has / introduced as the Money of Account. — Also, Rules for computing / Interest in such Money, and sundry useful Tables respecting the Same. / To all which an Index is annexed. / By Samuel Freeman, Esq. / Compiler of the Town Officer, Probate Auxiliary, and American Clerk's / Magazine. / Published according to Act of Congress. / Printed at Boston, / by Isaiah Thomas and Ebenezer T. Andrews, / [Proprietors of the Work.] / Faust's Statue, no. 45, Newbury Street. / 1795. Pages, (3), single page numbered iv, 296. 20 cm.

106. A / Treatise / of the / Law of / Partnership. / By William Watson, / of Lincoln's Inn, Esq. / Societas jus quoddam fraternitatis in se habet. / Dig. Pro Socio, Leg. 63. / Albany: / printed by Charles R. and George Webster, / In the White House corner of State and Pearl-Streets. / Sold at the Albany Bookstore, corner of State and Pearl Streets, and at Spencer's Bookstore, Albany; by H. Gaine, T. Greenleaf, S. Camp- / bell, T. Allen, & T. & J. Swords, New–York;

Thomas & Andrews, / Boston; Wm. Young, M. Carey, R. Campbell, Philadelphia. / 1795. Pages, xvi, 17–368. 20½ cm. John Carter Brown Library. Pages 361–368 contain subscribers names. The John Carter Brown copy has laid in pages 361–368 with a variant list of subscribers, indicating the possible existence of another impression, not located.

107. A / System / of the / Laws / of the / State of Connecticut. / In six books. / By Zephaniah Swift. / Volume I. / Windham: printed by John Byrne, for the author. / 1795. Pages, (3), single leaf numbered vii, 452; a folding Table of Descents, copper plate, between pages 292 and 293. 21 cm.

1796

108. A / System / of the / Laws / of the / State of Connecticut. / In six books. / By Zephaniah Swift. / Volume II. / Windham: printed by John Byrne, for the author, / 1796. Pages, (3), iv–v, 479; (12), index and list of subscribers. 21 cm.

109. A comparative view of mild and sanguinary Laws; and the good effects of the former, exhibited in the present economy of the prisons of Philadelphia. By The Duke De Liancourt. [Philadelphia, 1796?] The second edition of this printed in London by Dartin and Harvey, 1796, states on the title page that the original was printed in Philadelphia.

110. A Chart of the law of inheritance of the State of North-Carolina, exhibiting an historical view of it as it stood at the first settlement of the country, the changes it has undergone, and its present state. Newbern: Printed by François-X. Martin, 1796. Evans, 30742.

111. A / Comparative View / of the / Constitutions / of the / Several States With Each Other, and With That / Of The United States: / exhibiting in / Tables / The prominent Features of each Constitution, / and classing together their most important provisions under the / several heads of administration; / with / Notes and Observations. / By William

Smith, of South Carolina, L.L.D. / and member of the Congress of the United States. / Dedicated to the People of the United States. / Philadelphia, / printed by John Thompson, and sold by all the boobsellers [*sic*] in the United States./ 1796. Pages, (6), 4; six tables, two of which are folding, numbered I–VI; 9–34. 24 cm. Another copy has the first five tables numbered I–V, the sixth being unnumbered.

112. An / Essay / on the / Law of Bailments. / By William Jones, Esq. / of the Middle Temple. / (*four lines from*) Q. Scaevola, apud Cic. de Offic. Lib. III. / From the Press / of Samuel Etheredge, / For John West, No. 75, / Cornhill, Boston. / 1796. Pages, (2), [3]–178; (1), containing The Cases. 17 cm.

113. A / Treatise / on the / Jurisdiction and Proceedings / of / Justices of the Peace / in Civil Suits. / With an / Appendix, / containing / Advice to / Executors, Administrators and Guar- / dians. / Also an Epitome of the Law of / Landlord and Tenant; / The Whole interspersed with / Proper Forms, / And calculated for General Instruction. / By Wm. Griffith Esq. Counsellor at Law. / Burlington, / printed by Elderkin & Miller, 1796. Pages, (11), 272, (21). 17½ cm.

114. Defence of Usury; / shewing the / impolicy of the present legal re- / staints [*sic*] on the terms of / pecuniary bargains. / To which is added, / a letter / To Adam Smith, Esq. L.L.D. / on the / Discouragement of Inventive Industry. / By Jeremy Bentham, Esq. / of Lincoln's Inn. / Philadelphia: / printed for Mathew Carey, / By Lang and Ustick. / M.DCC.XCVI. Pages, (5), 6–149; (2), containing advertisements of books. 15 cm.

115. The / South-Carolina / Justice of Peace, / containing all the / duties, powers and authorities of that office, as re- / gulated by the laws now in force in this state. / And / Adapted to the Parish and County Magistrate. / To which is added, a great variety of / Warrants, Indictments and other precedents with several additional / ones interspersed under their several Heads, / and an addition / of several other decisions which have been had / in the courts of this state besides those / contained in the first edition. / The Second Edition, / Entered in the Secretary's Office of the State of South-Carolina, 11th October, 1788, agree- / able to the Act of Assembly in that Case made and provided, entitled "An Act for the En- / couragement of Arts and Sciences." Ratified the 26th March, 1784. / Peter Freneau, Secretary. / Philadelphia: Printed by R. Aitken & Son, No. 22, Market Street. / M.DCC.XCVI. Pages, viii, 641, (3). 20½ cm.

116. The / Law of Nations: / or, / Principles / of the / Law of Nature; / applied to the conduct and affairs / of / Nations And Sovereigns. / A Work tending to Display the True Interest of Power. / By M. De Vattel. / First American Edition, / Corrected and Revised from the latest London Edition. / (*three lines from*) Cicer. Somn. Scipion. / Translated from the French. / New-York: / Printed and sold by Samuel Campbell, 124 Pearl-street, / 1796. Pages, xlviii, (1), 50–563. 19 cm.

117. The / Poor Man's / Companion; / or / Miscellaneous Observations, / Concerning Penal and San- / guinary Laws, The Mode / and Nature of Evidence, / And, An Inquiry Into / The Propriety and / Policy of Punish- / ment. / By John Young, Esq. / Of Newhampshire, in / New-England. / Newbury, (Vermont) / Printed by Nathaniel Coverly, / And sold at his Bookstore, / Near the Court-House. Pages, (5), 6–100. Copyrighted October 20, 1796. 15½ cm. American Antiquarian Society.

118. A Visit to the Philadelphia Prison; being an accurate and particular account of the wise and humane administration adopted in every part of that building; containing also An Account of the Gradual Reformation, and Present Improved State, of the Penal Laws of Pennsylvania, with Observations on the Impolicy and Injustice of Capital Punishments. In a Letter to a Friend. By Robert J. Turnbull. "Vitiorum femina — otium — labore ex hauriendum." Lay then the axe to the root, and teach governments humanity. It is their sanguinary punishments which corrupt mankind. Rights of Man. Philadelphia: Printed by Budd and Bartram, No. 58, North Second Street. M.DCC.XCVI. Pages, iv, 108. 21 cm. N. Y. Public Library.

119. On the / prisons / of / Philadelphia. / By an European. / Philadelphia: / Printed and sold by Moreau de Saint-Mery, / Printer & Bookseller, No. 84, South Front-Street. / January 1796. 8vo. Pages, 46. American Antiquarian Society.

1797

120. A / Valuable Assistant to Every Man: / or, the / American Clerk's Magazine. / Containing the most Useful and Necessary / Forms of Writings, / Which commonly occur between Man and Man, under / the Names of / (*triple columns*) Acquittances, / Agreements, / Assignments, / Awards, / Bargains, / Bills, / Bonds, / Complaints, / Conveyances, / Covenants, / Deeds, / Feoffments, / Fine and Recovery, / Gifts, and Grants, / Indentures, / Leases, / Lease and Release, / Letters of Attor- / ney, / Mortgages, / Notes, / Pleas, / Petitions, / Receipts, / Releases, / Sales, / Surrenders, / Wills, / Writs and Dec- / larations, &c. / And other Instruments. / The whole of which are calculated for the / Use of the Citizens of the United States. / And are conformable to Law. / By Samuel Freeman, Esq. / Compiler of the Town Officer, Probate Auxiliary, and Massachusetts Justice. / The Third Edition, / revised, enlarged, and much improved. / Published according to Act of Congress. / Printed at Boston. / By I. Thomas and E. T. Andrews. / Sold by them at Faust's Statue, No. 45, Newbury-Street; by Thom- / as, Son & Thomas in Worcester; by Thomas, Andrews, / & Penniman, Albany; and by Thomas, Andrews / & Butler. Baltimore. — Feb. 1797. Pages, (3), single page numbered iv, (3), 8–297, (1). 17½ cm.

121. A / Treatise / on the / jurisdiction and proceedings / of / justices of the peace, / in civil suits; / with an / Appendix, / containing / Advice to Executors, Administrators and / Guardians — Also, an Epitome of the Law / of Landlord and Tenant; the whole / interspersed with proper forms, and / calculated for general instruction. / By Wm. Griffith, Esq. Counsellor at Law. / The second edition, with improvements, and a / new chapter on Conveyancing. / Newark, New-Jersey, / printed by John Woods, / For the Author. / M:DCC:XCVII. / Second title page: Part III. / The Scrivener's Guide; / containing / concise precedents of / Acquittances, Deeds of sale, partition, &c. / Agreements, Indentures of Apprentice, / Arbitration and Awards, Leases, / Assignments, Licence of Debtors, / Attornies Letters, &c. Mortgages, / Bills of Sale, Promissory notes, bills, &c. / Bonds and Conditions, Recognizance, / Composition with creditors, Wills and Codicils, / With practical Notes and Explanations. / "Multum in Parvo." Pages, (12), 273; (3), blank; second title page, verso blank; (1), advertisement, dated 20th May, 1797, verso blank; [277]–320; index, (21). 17 cm.

122. The / Scriveners Guide; / containing / concise precedents of / Acquittances, Deeds of sale, partition, &c. / Agreements, Indentures of Apprentice, / Arbitration and Awards, Leases, / Assignments, Licence of Debtors, / Attornies Letters, &c. Mortgages, / Bills of Sale, Promissory notes, bills, &c. / Bonds and Conditions, Recognizance, / Composition with creditors, Wills and Codicils, / With practical Notes and Explanations. / "Multum in Parvo." / By Wm. Griffith, Esq. Counsellor at Law. / Newark, New-Jersey, printed by John Woods. / M:DCC:XCVII. Pages, title page, verso blank; (1), advertisement dated 20th May, 1797, verso blank; [5]–48. 17 cm. Evans, 32212, says that this is a repaged reprint of pages 273–320 of the preceding.

123. The / Duty / of / Executors and Administrators: / pointing out, in a plain and familiar manner, how / executors are to proceed in the probate of / wills, getting in the effects, and / paying the debts and legacies / of their testator: /

shewing also who are entitled by law to be the / administrators of an intestate person: / With full and clear Directions to a Man's Relations how his Estate will / be distributed among them, according to the / Laws Of South-Carolina. / To which are prefixed, / all the / Statutes And Acts / relative to these subjects, / Mr. Blackstone's Rules For Interpreting / Wills And Deeds, / and / A Table Of Inheritance, / with a concise and easy explanation thereof. / To which is added, / A variety of Precedents of Wills, Codicils, &c. / with instructions for every person to make, alter / and republish his will; / and likewise, / All the Forms made use of in the Court of Ordinary. / Lex (de quâ agimus) est fons aequitatis. Cicero. / New-York: / Printed by T. and J. Swords, No. 99 Pearl-street. / 1797. Pages, (3), iv–xvii, 343; (1), containing copyright notice of deposit of title of book by John Faucheraud Grimké; (1), errata. Table between pages 288 and 289; A Table of Inheritance agreeable to the Act of Assembly, passed the 19th of February, 1791, (folding) between pages 300 and 301. 21 cm.

124. Half title: A / Treatise / on the / Police / of / London. / (title page) A / Treatise / on the / Police of London; / containing / A Detail / of the various / Crimes and Misdemeanors / by which public and private property and security are, at / present, injured and endangered: / and suggesting / Remedies for their Prevention. / The first American edition. / By A Magistrate. / Acting for the Counties of Middlesex, Surry, Kent, and Essex. — For the City and / Liberty of Westminster — and for the Liberty of the Tower of London. / (*five lines of Latin.*) / Philadelphia: / Printed for Benjamin Davies, No. 68, High-street. / by Henry Sweitzer, No. 85, Race-street, / MDCCXCVIII. Pages, (5), vi–xiv, (6), 342, xxiv; a folding table, A Summary View of the Prisoners committed, tried, punished, disposed of, and discharged in the Metropolis, in One / Year, ending in October, 1795. /, between pages 178 and 179. 21 cm.

125. The / Englishman's Right, / or, / A Dialogue / between a / Barrister at Law and a Juryman; / shewing, /

(*double columns*) 1. The Antiquity. / 2. The Excellent designed Use. / 3. The Office and just Privileges of / Juries by the Law of England. / (Being a Choice Help for all who are qualified by Law, / to serve on Juries) / By Sir John Hawles, Knt. / solicitor general to the late King William. / To which is prefixed, / An Introductory Essay, on the Moral Duty of a Judge. / by Lord Bacon. / Honestissimum enim est majorum vestigia sequi, si modo recto / itinere praecesserint. Plin, lib. V epist. 4. / Printed by John Thompson, of Philadelphia; / for Alexander Brodie, / 1798. Pages, (4), 5–6, (1); single page numbered viii, (1), 18–70. 19½ cm.

126. A / Treatise / on the / Law / of / Bills of Exchange / and / Promissory Notes. / By / Stewart Kyd, of the Middle Temple, esq. / barrister at law. / The First American, / From the Third London, Edition. / With considerable additions. / Boston: / Printed by Manning & Loring, / For S. Hall, W. Spotswood, J. White, / Thomas & Andrews, D. West, / E. Larkin, W. P. & L. Blake, / and J. West, / 1798. Pages, (4), v–xii, 288. 17½ cm.

127. Another edition of the above. The title pages are identical with the exception of the following: Boston : / Printed by Manning & Loring, / For David West, Sold at his Bookstore, / No. 56, Cornhill: by Ebenezer S. Thomas, Charles- / ton, South-Carolina; and by Solomon Cotton & / Co. Baltimore, / 1798. Pages, (4), v–xii, 288. 17½ cm. Page 35 is numbered 36; page 49 is numbered 4; page 93 is numbered 39.

128. The / Civil and Executive / Officer's Assistant; / containing the forms of / (*double columns*) Bonds, / Bills, / Deeds, / Letters of Attorney, / Policies of Insurance, / Releases, / Wills, / Writs, / Pleas, / Officer's Returns, and / Justices Records of / Courrt [*sic*]. / With the power and duty of / Justices of the Peace, / as contained in the laws of the state of / Connecticut, / and exhibiting the duty and province of / Select-men, Constables, Grand-jurors, &c. / With an / Appendix, / containing a concise mode of casting interest, / keeping town accompts, and transacting pub- / lic business with facility and accuracy. / By John Goodrich, esq. / The second edition, / revised, corrected, and considerably enlarged, / Published according to Act of Congress. / Hartford: printed by Hudson & Goodwin. / M,DCC,XCVIII. Pages, (3), iv–xii, 239. 17½ cm. Connecticut State Library.

1799

129. Commentaries / on the / Laws of England. / In four books. / By / Sir William Blackstone, Knt. / one of the late Justices of his Brittanic Majesty's / Court of Common Pleas. / In four volumes. / Second American Edition, / Carefully reprinted from the last London Edition. / Containing / the Last Corrections of the Author, / the Additions by Richard Burn, LL.D. / and Continued to the Present Time, / by John Williams, Esq. / Vol. I — Book I. / Printed at Boston, / by I. Thomas and E. T. Andrews, / Sold by them at Faust's Statue, No. 45, Newbury-Street; by I. / Thomas, Worcester; by Thomas, Andrews, and Penniman, / Albany; by Thomas, Andrews, and Butler, Balti- / more; and by E. S. Thomas, Charleston, S. C. / 1799. The title pages and size of the four volumes are identical, with the exception of volume and book number.

Vol. I — Book I. Pages, (1), portrait, engraved by S. Hill; (3); single page numbered iv; (3); single page numbered 3; (1), half title: Introduction. / Of the / Study, Nature, and Extent / of the / Laws of England. / , verso blank; (1), 4–512. 17 cm. At the end of Vol. I, with separate title page and pagination, is bound in Edward Christian's Notes, printed at Boston, by Thomas and Andrews, 1801, 123 pages.

Vol. II — Book II. Pages, (3), iv–vi, 520, xviii; 79, Mr. Christian's Notes. Table of consanguinity inserted between pages 202 and 203 and a folding Table of Descents between pages 240 and 241.

Vol. III. — Book III. Pages, (3), iv–vi, [1]–60; 59*–60*; 61–166; 165*–166*, 167–411, 410*–411*, 412–455, xxviii; 32, Mr. Christian's Notes. Page 71 is misnumbered 17.

Vol. IV — Book IV. Pages, (3), iv–vi, [1]–160, 159*–162*, 161–236, 235*–236*, 237–374, 373*–374*, 375–442, vi; (52), Index; 38, Mr. Christian's Notes. Page 79 is misnumbered 97 and page 267, 167.

130. The / Town Officer: / or the / Power and Duty of / (*double columns*) Selectmen, / Town Clerks, / Town Treasurers, / Overseers of the Poor, / Assessors, / Constables, / Collectors of Taxes, / Surveyors of Highways, / Surveyors of Lumber, / Fence Viewers, / Clerks of the Market, / Measurers of Wood, / And other Town Officers. / As contained in the / Laws of the Commonwealth of Massachusetts. / With a / Variety of Forms, / for the Use of such Officers. / To which are added, / The Power and Duty of / Towns, Parishes and Plantations, / and a / Plain and regular Method to Keep Accounts / of the Expenditures of Monies voted by a / Town; upon an Inspection of which, the State of its / Finances may at any Time be Known. / The Fourth Edition. / Much improved, and greatly enlarged. / By Samuel Freeman, esq. / Author of the Massachusetts Justice, Probate Auxiliary, and American Clerk's / Magazine. / Published according to Act of Congress. / Printed at Boston, / by I. Thomas and E. T. Andrews, / proprietors of the work, / Faust's Statue, No. 45, Newbury Street. / Feb. 1799. Pages, (3), iv, (3), 8–287. 17 cm.

131. The / New Virginia Justice / comprising the / Office and Authority / of a / Justice of the Peace, / in the / Commonwealth of Virginia. / Together / with a variety of useful precedents adapted to / the Laws now in force. / To which is added, / an Appendix containing all the most approved / forms of conveyancing, commonly used in this / country, such as deeds, of bargain and sale, / of lease and release, of trust, mort- / gages, &c. — Also the duties of a / Justice of the Peace, aris- / ing under the laws of the / United States. / By William Waller Hening, / attorney at law. / Richmond — printed by Aug; Davis. / MDCCXIX. Pages, (12), 468; Appendix No. I. / to the / New Virginia Justice, &c. / containing / Forms of Conveyancing. / (2), iii–xxiv; Appendix

No. II. / to the / New Virginia Justice, &c. / containing / The Duties of a Justice of the Peace, / arising under the laws of the United States. /, (1), 2–32; index (1), ii–xv. 20½ cm.

132. A / System of the Law / of / Marine Insurances. / With three chapters / On Bottomry; / On Insurances On Lives; / and / On Insurances Against Fire. / By James Allan Park, / of Lincoln's Inn, esq. barrister at law. / Lex (de quâ agimus) est fons aequitatis. Cicero. / Second American, from the latest English, / edition. / Printed at Boston, / For Thomas and Andrews, No. 45, Newbury-street, / David West, No. 56, / And John West, No. 75, Cornhill. / Sold at their several Bookstores. / Aug. 1799. Pages, (3), iv–xxvii, liv; [502], irregularly paged, 449–516. 23 cm.

1800

133. The / Clerk's Magazine: / Containing the most Useful and Necessary / Forms of Writings, / Which commonly occur between Man and Man, / under the names of / (*triple columns*) Acquittances, / Agreements, / Assignments, / Awards, / Bargains, / Bills, / Bonds, / Conveyances, / Covenants, / Deeds, / Declarations, / Exchanges, / Gifts and Grants, / Indentures, / Leases, / Letters of Attor- / ney, / Livery and Seisin, / Mortgages, / Noles [*sic*], Pleas, / Petitions, / Receipts, / Releases, / Sales, / Surrenders, / Wills, / Writs, &c. &c. / And other Instruments. / Calculated for the / Use of the Citizens of the United States. / To which is added, / The Constitution of the United States, / and Amendments thereto; / The Constitution of the State of New-York; / An Act of Congress prescribing the mode in which the Public / Acts, Records and Judicial Proceedings in each State shall be / authenticated, so as to take effect in every other State; / An Act respecting the Electors of a President of the United States; / The Money of Accounts of the State of New-York; / Together with a Schedule of the whole Number of Inhabitants / in the United States, and in the several Counties of this State. / Albany: / Printed by Charles R. and George Webster, / and sold at their Bookstore, corner of State and Pearl-streets. / and by Daniel

Steele, corner of Hudson and Court-streets. Pages, (4), 310, (6). 17 cm. American Antiquarian Society. Preface To the Public, dated, Albany, 1st August, 1800.

134. A / System of the Law / of / Marine Insurances. / With three chapters / On Bottomry; / On Insurances On Lives; / and / On Insurances Against Fire. / By James Allan Park, / of Lincoln's Inn, esq. barrister at law. / Lex (de quâ agimus) est fons aequitatis. Cicero. / Third American, From The Latest English, / Edition. / Printed at Boston, / For Thomas and Andrews, No. 45, Newbury-Street, / David West, No. 56, / And John West, No. 75, Cornhill. / Sold at their several Bookstores. / 1800. Pages, (3), iv–xxvii, (1), ii–liv, (511), irregularly paged, 459–516. 23 cm.

135. A / System of the Law / of / Marine Insurances. / With three chapters / On Bottomry; / On Insurances On Lives; / and / On Insurances Against Fire. / By James Allan Park, / of Lincoln's Inn, esq. barrister at law. / Lex (de quâ agimus) est fons aequitatis. Cicero. / Second American, from the third English edition. / To which is added, in / An Appendix, / all the / New Cases added to the Fourth English Edition, / Printed in 1800, / Many Of Which Are Important. / Printed at Boston, / For Thomas and Andrews, No. 45, Newbury-Street, / David West, No. 56, / And John West, No. 75, Cornhill. / Sold at their several Bookstores. / 1800. As the pagination is identical with the preceding, probably the sheets of the previous edition with a new title page and an appendix: Appendix / to / A System of the Law / of / Marine Insurances. / By James Allan Park, / of Lincoln's Inn, esq. barrister at law. / Containing all the / New Cases added to the Fourth English Edition, / Printed in 1800, / Many Of Which Are Important. / Printed at Boston, / For Thomas and Andrews, No. 45, Newbury-Street, / David West, No. 56, / And John West, No. 75, Cornhill. / Sold at their several Bookstores. / 1800. Pages, (4); single page numbered v; verso blank; (32), irregularly paged.

136. A / System of the Law / of / Marine Insurances. / With three chapters / On Bottomry; / On Insurances On

Lives; / and / On Insurances Against Fire. / By James Allan Park, / of Lincoln's Inn, esq. barrister at law. / Lex (de quâ agimus) est fons aequitatis. Cicero. / Third American, from the Third English edition. / To which is added, in / An Appendix, / all the / New Cases added to the Fourth English Edition, / Printed in 1800, / Many Of Which Are Important. / Printed at Boston, / For Thomas and Andrews, No. 45, Newbury-Street, / David West, No. 56, / And John West, No. 75, Cornhill. / Sold at their several Bookstores. / 1800. Followed by title page of American edition of Aug. 1799. With exception of these two title pages, exactly the same as the foregoing.

137. A / Valuable Assistant to Every Man: / or, the / American Clerk's Magazine. / Containing the most Useful and Necessary / Forms of Writings, / Which commonly occur between Man and Man, under the / Names of / (*triple columns*) Acquittances, / Agreements, / Awards, / Bargains, / Bills, / Bonds, / Complaints, / Conveyances, / Covenants, / Deeds, / Feoffments, / Fine and Recovery, / Gifts and Grants, / Indentures, / Leases, / Lease and Release, / Letters of Attorney, / Mortgages, / Notes, / Pleas, / Petitions, / Probate Matters, / Receipts, / Releases, / Sales, / Surrenders, / Wills, / Writs and Dec- / larations, &c. / and other Instruments. / The whole of which are calculated for the / Use of the Citizens of the United States. / And are conformable to Law. / By Samuel Freeman, Esq. / Compiler of the Town Officer, Probate Auxiliary, and Massachusetts Justice. / The Fourth Edition, / revised and improved. / Published according to Act of Congress. / Printed at Boston, / By I. Thomas and E. T. Andrews. / Sold by them at Faust's Statue, No. 45, Newbury Street; by I. / Thomas, Worcester; by Thomas, Andrews & Penniman, / Albany; and by Thomas, Andrews, & Butler, / Baltimore. — April, 1800. Pages, (3), single page numbered iv, (3), 8–303, (1). 16½ cm.

138. A / Treatise / on the / Law / of / Bills Of Exchange / and / Promissory Notes. / By / Stewart Kyd, of the Middle

Temple, esq. / barrister at law. / The Second American, / From The Third London, Edition. / With considerable additions. / Albany: / Printed by Loring Andrews, / For Thomas, Andrews & Penniman, / sold by them at their Store, No. 45, State-street, Albany, / by Isaiah Thomas, at Worcester, Massachusetts, / by Thomas & Andrews, at Boston, / and by Thomas, Andrews & Butler, at Baltimore, / Maryland. / 1800. Pages, (4), v–xii, 288. 16 cm.

139. The / General Instructor: / or the / Office, Duty, And Authority / of / Justices Of The Peace, Sheriffs, Coroners And Constables, / in the / State of Kentucky. / With Precedents suited to every case that can pos- / sibly arise in either of those Offices, under the / Laws now in force, with references to the Laws out of which they do arise. / The whole Alphabetically digested under the se- / veral Titles; with an Index for the ready find- / ing any Matter sought. / By John Bradford. / Lexington: / Printed by John Bradford on Main Street. / 1800. Pages, (5), vi–xii, 252. 18 cm.

140. A / Practical Treatise / upon the / Bankrupt Law / of the / United States. / By R. Fields. / Attorney At Law. / Copy Right Secured. / Boston: Printed by B. Edes & Son./ — 1800. — Pages, (3), 4–59. 19 cm.

141. The / Duty and Office / of / Justices of Peace, / and of/ Sheriffs, Coroners, Constables, &c. / According to the Laws of the State of North Carolina. / To which is added / An Appendix, / Containing the Act directing the Mode of recovering Debts / of twenty Pounds and under; the Declaration of Rights / and Constitution of this State; the Constitution of / the United States, with the Amendments / thereto; and an Abstract from the Act of / Congress, laying Duties on stamped / Vellum, Parchment and Paper. / Together with / A Collection of the most useful Precedents. / By John Haywood, Esquire. / Late one of the Judges of the Superior Courts of Law and Equity. / Halifax: / Printed by Abraham Hodge. / M.DCCC. Pages, (3), iv–viii, 400. 20½ cm.

REPRINTS OF LEGAL CLASSICS PUBLISHED BY THE LAWBOOK EXCHANGE, LTD.

ADMIRALTY AND MARITIME LAW

Ashburner, Walter. *The Rhodian Sea-Laws. Edited from the Manuscripts.* Oxford: Clarendon Press, 1909. ccxciii, 132 pp. Reprinted 2001 by The Lawbook Exchange, Ltd. LCCN 00-065551. ISBN 1-58477-173-9. Cloth. $75.

Benedict, Erastus C. *The American Admiralty: Its Jurisdiction and Practice with Practical Forms and Directions.* New York: Banks, Gould & Co., 1850. xiii, 651 pp. Reprinted 2002 by the Lawbook Exchange, Ltd. LCCN 2991941402. ISBN 1-58477-191-7. Cloth. $110.

Browne, Arthur. *A Compendious View of the Civil Law and of the Law of the Admiralty: being the substance of a course of lectures read in the University of Dublin.* New York: Halstead and Voorhies, 1840. Two volumes. xvi, 536; xi, 567 pp. Reprinted 2000 by The Lawbook Exchange, Ltd. LCCN 99-18284. ISBN 1-886363-88-9. Cloth. $175.

Flanders, Henry. *A Treatise on Maritime Law.* Boston: Little, Brown and Company, 1852. xvi, 444 pp. Reprinted 1999 by The Lawbook Exchange, Ltd. ISBN 1-886363-72-2. Cloth. $75.

Fulton, Thomas Wemyss. *The Sovereignty of the Sea.* Edinburgh: William Blackwood and Sons, 1911. xxvi, 799 pp. Illustrated. Reprint available 2002 by The Lawbook Exchange, Ltd. ISBN 1-58477-232-8. Cloth. $110.

Johnson, Hebert Alan. *The Law Merchant and Negotiable Instruments in Colonial New York, 1664 to 1730.* Chicago: Loyola University Press, 1963. Reprint available 2002 by The Lawbook Exchange, Ltd. LCCN 2001037701. ISBN 1-58477-208-5. Cloth. $60.

Kulsrud, Carl J. *Maritime Neutrality to 1780. A History of the Main Principles Governing Neutrality and Belligerency to 1780.* Boston: Little, Brown, and Company, 1936. x, 351 pp. Reprinted 2000 by The Lawbook Exchange, Ltd. LCCN 99-38825. ISBN 1-58477-027-9. Cloth. $65.

Marsden. R.[eginald]. G.[odfrey], ed. *Documents Relating to Law and Custom of the Sea.* [n.p.]: The Navy Record Society, 1915-6. Two volumes. xxxiii, 561; xl, 457, [5] pp. Reprinted 1999 by The Lawbook Exchange, Ltd. LCCN 99-24138. ISBN 1-886363-96-X. Cloth. $175.

Twiss, Sir Travers]. *The Black Book of the Admiralty, with an Appendix.* Monumenta Juridica. Edited by Sir Travers Twiss. Four volumes. 4, xciii, 491, [2]; 4, lxxxvii, 500, 31; 4, lxxxvi, 673, [1], 31; 4, clii, 559, 32 pp. LCCN 97-38809 ISBN 1-886363-39-0. 1871. Reprinted 1998 by The Lawbook Exchange, Ltd. Cloth. $495.

ANCIENT, ROMAN AND GREEK LAW

Berger, Adolf. *Encyclopedic Dictionary of Roman Law.* Philadelphia: The American Philosophical Society, [1953]. (Transactions of the American Philosophical Society; new series, volume 43, part 2, 1953). [ii], 333-808 pp. Reprinted 2002 by The Lawbook Exchange, Ltd. LCCN 00-067774. ISBN 1-58477-142-9. Cloth. $110.

Bonner, Robert J. and Gertrude Smith. *The Administration of Justice from Homer to Aristotle.* Chicago: The University of Chicago Press, [1930]. Two volumes. ix, 390; vii, [320] pp. Reprinted 2001 by The Lawbook Exchange, Ltd. ISBN 1-58477-117-8. Cloth. $160.

Botsford, George Willis. *The Roman Assemblies from their Origin to the End of the Republic.* New York: The Macmillan Company, 1909. x, 521 pp. Reprinted 2001 by The Lawbook Exchange, Ltd. ISBN 1-58477-165-8. Cloth. $85.

Buckland, W.W. *The Roman Law of Slavery: The Condition of the Slave in Private Law from Augustus to Justinian.* Cambridge: Cambridge University Press, 1908. xii, [2], 735 pp. Reprinted 2001 by The Lawbook Exchange, Ltd. LCCN 99-056922. ISBN 1-58477-068-6. Cloth. $175.

Bussell, F.W. *The Roman Empire. Essays on the Constitutional History from the Accession of Domitian (81 A.D.) to the Retirement of Nicephorus III. (1081 A.D.)* London: Longmans, Green, and Co., 1910. Two volumes. xiv, 402; xxiii, 521 pp. Reprinted 2000 by The Lawbook Exchange, Ltd. LCCN 99-087026. ISBN 1-58477-082-1. Cloth. $175.

Girard, Paul F. *A Short History of Roman Law. Being the First Part of his Manuel Elementaire De Droit Romain. Translated by Augustus Henry Frazer and John Home Cameron.* Toronto: Canada Law Book Company, 1906, v, 220 pp. Reprinted 2000 by The Lawbook Exchange, Ltd. LCCN 99-087383. ISBN 1-58477-078-3. Cloth. $55.

Greenidge, A.H.J. *The Legal Procedure of Cicero's Time.* Oxford: The Clarendon Press, 1901. xiii, 599 pp. Reprinted 2000 by The Lawbook Exchange, Ltd. LCCN 99-26771. ISBN 1-886363-99-4. Cloth. $85.

Harper, Robert Francis. *The Code of Hammurabi King of Babylon. About 2250 B.C. Autographed Text transliteration...* Chicago: The

University of Chicago Press, 1904. xxviii, 194, ciii (plates) pp. Illus. Reprinted 2000 The Lawbook Exchange, Ltd. LCCN 99-23953. ISBN 1-58477-003-1. Cloth. $75.

Jackson, E. Hilton. *Latin for Lawyers. Containing I: A Course in Latin, with Legal Maxims and Phrases As a Basis of Instruction. II. A Collection of Over One Thousand Latin Maxims, with English Translations, Explanatory Notes, and Cross-References. III. A Vocabulary of Latin Words.* London: Sweet & Maxwell, 1915. viii, 300 pp. Reprinted 1992 by The Lawbook Exchange, Ltd. LCCN 92-074408. ISBN 0-9630106-4-6. Cloth. $50.

Johns, C.H.W. *Babylonian and Assyrian Laws, Contracts and Letters.* Edinburgh: T. & T. Clark, 1904. xxii, 424 pp. Reprinted 2000 by The Lawbook Exchange, Ltd. LCCN 99-32862. ISBN 1-58477-022-8. Cloth. $75.

Johns, C.H.W. , translator. *The Oldest Code of Laws in the World: The Code of Laws Promulgated by Hammurabi, King of Babylon, B.C. 2285-2242.* Edinburgh: T. & T. Clark, 1926. xii, 88 pp. Reprinted 2000 by The Lawbook Exchange, Ltd. LCCN 99-053070. ISBN 1-58477-061-9. Cloth. $60.

Mendelsohn, S. *The Criminal Jurisprudence of the Ancient Hebrews. Compiled from the Talmud and other Rabbinical Writings, and Compared with Roman and English Penal Jurisprudence.* Baltimore: M. Curlander, 1891. 270 pp. Reprint available 2002 by The Lawbook Exchange, Ltd. ISBN 1-58477-150-X. Cloth. $80.

Moyle, J.B. *The Institutes of Justinian.* Translated into English with an Index. Fifth Edition. Oxford: Clarendon Press, 1913. viii, 220 pp. Reprint available 2002 by The Lawbook Exchange, Ltd. LCCN 2001041401. ISBN 1-58477-185-2. Cloth. $75.

Pharr, Clyde. *The Theodosian Code and Novels and the Sirmondian Constitutions. A Translation with Commentary, Glossary, and Bibliography.* [Princeton]: Princeton University Press, 1952. Quarto. Book measures 9"x12." xxvi, 643 pp. Reprinted 2001 by The Lawbook Exchange, Ltd. ISBN 1-58477-146-1. Cloth. $150.

Roby, Henry John. *An Introduction to the Study of Justinian's Digest Containing an Account of its Composition and of the Jurists Used or Referred to Therein.* Cambridge: At the University Press, 1886. cclxxix pp. Reprinted 2000 by The Lawbook Exchange, Ltd. ISBN 1-58477-073-2. Cloth. $65.

Roby, Henry John. *Roman Private Law in the Times of Cicero and of the Antonines.* Cambridge: At the University Press, 1902. Two volumes. xxxii, 543; xiii, [1], 560 pp. Reprinted 2000 by The Lawbook

Exchange, Ltd. ISBN 1-58477-074-0. Cloth. $180.

Sandys, Sir John Edwin. *Aristotle's Constitution of Athens. A Revised Text with an Introduction Critical and Explanatory Notes Testimonia and Indices. Second edition, Revised and Enlarged.* London: Macmillan & Co., Limited, 1902. xcii, 331 pp. Frontis. Illus. Reprinted 2000 by The Lawbook Exchange, Ltd. LCCN 99-23952. ISBN 1-58477-004-X. Cloth. $75.

Scott, S.P. *The Civil Law Including the Twelve Tables, The Institutes of Gaius, The Rules of Ulpian, the Opinions of Paulus, The Enactments of Justinian, and the Constitutions of Leo: Translated from the original Latin, edited, and compared with all accessible systems of jurisprudence ancient and modern. In Seventeen Volumes. In seven books.* Cincinnati: The Central Trust Company, 1932. Reprinted 2001 by The Lawbook Exchange, Ltd. ISBN 1-58477-130-5. Cloth. $895.

Vinogradoff, Paul. *Roman Law in Mediaeval Europe.* London: Harper & Brothers, 1909. 136 pp. Reprinted 2001 by The Lawbook Exchange, Ltd. LCCN 00-039068. ISBN 1-58477-109-7. Cloth. $65.

BIBLICAL AND CANON LAW

Clark, H.B. *Biblical Law: Being a text of the statutes, ordinances, and judgments established in the Holy Bible-with many allusions to secular laws-ancient, medieval, and modern-documented to the Scriptures, judicial decisions, and legal literature.* Portland, Ore.: Binfords & Mort, [1943]. xxiv, 304 pp. Reprinted 2000 by The Lawbook Exchange, Ltd. LCCN 99-053316. ISBN 1-58477-062-7. Cloth. $75.

Ehrlich, J.W. *The Holy Bible and the Law.* New York: Oceana Publications, [1962]. 240 pp. Reprint available 2002 by The Lawbook Exchange, Ltd. LCCN 2001041307. ISBN 1-58477-192-5. Cloth. $75.

Friedberg, Emil Albert and Aemilius Ludwig Richter. *Corpus iuris canonici.-Editio Lipsiensis secunda / post Aemilii Ludouici Richteri curas ad librorum manu scriptorum et editionis Romanae fidem recognouit et adnotatione critica instruxit Aemilius Friedberg.* Liepzig : Tauchnitz, 1879-1881. Two volumes. civ, 1472 columns (736 pp.); lxxxii, 1340 columns (670 pp.) LCCN 99-088231. Reprinted 2000 by The Lawbook Exchange, Ltd. LCCN 99-088231. ISBN 1-58477-088-0. Cloth. $300.

Goodenough, Edwin R. *The Jurisprudence of the Jewish Courts in Egypt: Legal Administration by the Jews under the Early Roman Empire as Described by Philo Judaeus.* New Haven: Yale University Press, 1929. vii, 268 pp. Reprint available 2002 by The Lawbook Exchange, Ltd. ISBN 1-58477-152-6. Cloth. $75.

Goodhart, Arthur L. *Five Jewish Lawyers of the Common Law.* London: Oxford University Press, 1949. [4], 74 pp. Reprinted 2000 by The Lawbook Exchange, Ltd. LCCN 99-049934. ISBN 1-58477-045-7. Cloth. $60.

Greenleaf, Simon. *The Testimony of the Evangelists Examined by the Rules of Evidence Administered in Courts of Justice with an Appendix Containing a History of the Most Ancient Manuscript Copies of the New Testament, and a Comparison of their Text with that of the King James' Bible by Constantine Tischendorff. Also a Review of the Trial of Jesus.* New York: James Cockcroft & Company, 1874. Reprinted 2001 by The Lawbook Exchange, Ltd.xxiii, 613 pp. LCCN 00-021510. ISBN 1-58477-095-3. Cloth. $95.

Jackson, E. Hilton. *Latin for Lawyers. Containing I: A Course in Latin, with Legal Maxims and Phrases As a Basis of Instruction. II. A Collection of Over One Thousand Latin Maxims, with English Translations, Explanatory Notes, and Cross-References. III. A Vocabulary of Latin Words.* London: Sweet & Maxwell, 1915. viii, 300 pp. Reprinted 1992 by The Lawbook Exchange, Ltd. LCCN 92-074408. ISBN 0-9630106-4-6. Cloth. $50.

Maitland, Frederic William. *Roman Canon Law in the Church of England: Six Essays.* London: Methuen & Co., 1898. vii, 184 pp. Reprinted 1998 by The Lawbook Exchange, Ltd. LCCN 98-22357. ISBN 1-886363-57-9. Cloth. $65.

Mendelsohn, S. *The Criminal Jurisprudence of the Ancient Hebrews. Compiled from the Talmud and other Rabbinical Writings, and Compared with Roman and English Penal Jurisprudence.* Baltimore: M. Curlander, 1891. 270 pp. Reprint available 2002 by The Lawbook Exchange, Ltd. ISBN 1-58477-150-X. Cloth. $80.

Ogle, Arthur. *The Canon Law in Mediaeval England. An Examination of William Lyndwood's "Provinciale," in Reply to the Late Professor F.W. Maitland.* London: John Murray, 1912. xv, 220 pp. Reprinted 2000 by The Lawbook Exchange, Ltd. LCCN 99-33827. ISBN 1-58477-026-0. Cloth. $65.

Schulte, Joh. Friedrich von. *Die Geschichte der Quellen und Literatur der canonischen Rechts.* Stuttgart: Verlag von Ferdinand Enke, 1875. Two volumes. Reprinted 2000 by The Lawbook Exchange, Ltd. LCCN 99-087494. ISBN 1-58477-089-9. Cloth. $225.

Townley, James. *The Reasons of the Laws of Moses from the "More Nevochim" of Maimonides. With Notes, Dissertations, and a Life of the Author.* London: Longman, Rees, Orme, Brown, and Green, 1827. xi, 451 pp. Reprinted 2001 by The Lawbook Exchange, Ltd. ISBN 1-

58477-168-2. Cloth. $95.

White, Edw. J. *The Law in Scriptures. With Explanations of the Law Terms and Legal References in Both the Old and the New Testaments.* St. Louis: Thomas Law Book Company, 1935. xxiv, 422 pp. Reprinted 2000 by The Lawbook Exchange, Ltd. LCCN 99-059102. ISBN 1-58477-076-7. Cloth. $80.

LEGAL BIBLIOGRAPHY

Benedict, Russell. *Acts and Laws of the Thirteen Original Colonies and States: Constituting the extraordinary collection of Hon. Russell Benedict.* New York: American Art Association, 1922. [272]pp. Reprinted 1998 The Lawbook Exchange, Ltd. LC 98-20196 ISBN 1-886363-56-0. Cloth. $85.

[Blackstone, William]. Eller, Catherine Spicer. *The William Blackstone Collection in the Yale Law Library. A Bibliographical Catalogue.* New Haven: Yale University Press, 1938. xvii, 113 pp. Reprinted 1993 by The Lawbook Exchange, Ltd. LCCN 99-38826. ISBN 0-9630106-5-4. Cloth. $50.

DePuy, Henry F. *A Bibliography of the English Colonial Treaties with the American Indians.* New York: the Lenox Club, 1917. [108] pp. Reprinted 2001 by The Lawbook Exchange, Ltd. ISBN 1-58477-163-1. Cloth. $50.

Friend, Willam L. *Anglo-American Legal Bibliographies. An Annotated Guide.* Washington, D.C.: United States Government Printing Office, 1944. xii, 166 pp. Reprinted 1996 by The Lawbook Exchange, Ltd. LCCN 96-11002. ISBN 1-886363-21-8. Cloth. $65.

James, Eldon Revare. *A List of Legal Treatises Printed in the British Colonies and the American States Before 1801.* Cambridge, Mass.: Harvard University Press, 1934. 52 pp. Reprint available 2002 by The Lawbook Exchange, Ltd. ISBN 1-58477-143-7. Cloth. $50.

Marke, Julius J., editor. *A Catalogue of the Law Collection at New York University With Selected Annotations.* New York: The Law Center of New York University, 1953. xxxi, 1372 pp. Reprinted 1999 by The Lawbook Exchange, Ltd. LCCN 99-19939. ISBN 1-886363-91-9. Cloth. $185.

[Marshall, John]. Servies, James Albert. *A Bibliography of John Marshall.* Washington: United States Commission for the Celebration of the Two Hundredth Anniversary of the Birth of John Marshall, 1956. xix, 182 pp. Reprinted 2000 by The Lawbook Exchange, Ltd. LCCN 99-088239. ISBN 1-58477-083-X. Cloth. $65.

Maxwell, W. Harold and C.R. Brown. *A Complete List of British and Colonial Law Reports and Legal Periodicals. Arranged in Alphabetical and in Chronological Order with Bibliographical Notes.* **[With]:** *Check List of Canadian and Newfoundland Statutes.*[Third Edition]. Toronto: The Carswell Company, Limited, 1937. viii, 141, 49 pp. Reprinted 1995 by The Lawbook Exchange, Ltd. LCCN 96-14504. ISBN 1-886363-11-0. Cloth. $70.

Schroeder, Theodore. *Free Speech Bibliography Including Every Discovered Attitude Toward the Problem Covering Every Method of Transmitting Ideas and Abridging Their Promulgation upon Every Subject-Matter.* New York: The H.W. Wilson Company, 1922. [vii], 247 pp. Reprinted 2001 by The Lawbook Exchange, Ltd. LCCN 99-049361. ISBN 1-58477-053-8. Cloth. $85.

[Worrall, John and Edward Brooke]. *Bibliotheca Legum Angliae. Or, a Catalogue of the Common and Statute Law Books of This Realm, and Some Others Relating Thereto: Giving an Account of Their Several Editions, Ancient Printers, Dates, and Prices, and Wherein They Differ. [With a Supplement to 1800]. Part I Compiled by John Worrall, Part II and Supplement Compiled by Edward Brooke. Parts I, II and Supplement bound in one volume.* London: Printed for Edward Brooke, 1788-1800. [15], 272, [26]; viii, 40, 49-255, [1]; [3], 45, [2] pp. 1788-1800. Reprinted 1997 by The Lawbook Exchange, Ltd. LCCN 97-12962. ISBN 1-886363-29-3. Cloth. $110.

LEGAL BIOGRAPHY AND PERSONAGES

Adams, W.H. Davenport. *Learned in the Law; or Examples and Encouragements from the Lives of Eminent Lawyers.* London: S.W. Partridge & Co., [1882?]. vi, 392 pp. Reprint available 2002 by The Lawbook Exchange, Ltd. ISBN 1-58477-238-7. Cloth. $80.

Anthony, Susan B. *An Account of the Proceedings of the Trial of Susan B. Anthony, on the Charge of Illegal Voting, at the Presidential Election in Nov., 1872. and on the Trial of Beverly W. Jones, Edwin T. Marsh and William B. Hall, the Inspectors of Election by whom her Vote was Received.* Rochester: Daily Democrat and Chronicle Book Print, 1874. vii, 212 pp. Reprint available 2002 by The Lawbook Exchange, Ltd. LCCN 2001041397. ISBN 1-58477-187-9. Cloth. $65.

[Brandeis, Louis D.]. *Brandeis on Zionism. A Collection of Addresses and Statements by Louis D. Brandeis with a Foreword by Mr. Justice Felix Frankfurter.* Washington, D.C.: Zionist Organization of America, [1942]. viii, 156 pp. Reprinted 1999 by The Lawbook Exchange, Ltd. LCCN 98-49331. ISBN 1-886363-60-9. Cloth. $65.

Brightwell, C.L. *Memorials of the Early Lives and Doings of Great Lawyers.* London: T. Nelson and Sons, 1866. 251 pp. Reprint available 2002 by The Lawbook Exchange, Ltd. ISBN 1-58477-236-0. Cloth. $65.

Cameron, James R. *Frederick William Maitland and the History of English Law.* Norman: University of Oklahoma Press, [1961]. xvi, 214 pp. Portrait frontis. Illustrations. Reprinted 2001 by The Lawbook Exchange, Ltd. LCCN 00-067585. ISBN 1-58477-135-6. Cloth. $85.

[Cardozo, Benjamin]. *Law is Justice. Notable Opinions of Mr. Justice Cardozo.* Foreword by Robert F. Wagner. Edited by A.L. Sainer. New York: Ad Press Ltd., [1938]. xvii, 441 pp. Frontis. Reprinted 1999 by The Lawbook Exchange, Ltd. LCCN 99-34154. ISBN 1-58477-010-4. Cloth. $75.

Curtis, Benjamin R. *A Memoir of Benjamin Robbins Curtis, LL.D. with some of his Professional and Miscellaneous Writings.* Boston: Little Brown, and Company, 1879. Two volumes. Illustrated. Reprint available 2002 by The Lawbook Exchange, Ltd. ISBN 1-58477-235-2. Cloth. $175.

Darrow, Clarence and William J. Bryan. *The World's Most Famous Court Trial. Tennessee Evolution Case. A Complete Stenographic Report of the Famous Court Test of the Anti-Evolution Act, at Dayton July 10 to 21, 1925, Including Speeches and Arguments of Attorneys.* Cincinnati: National Book Company, [1925]. [4], 339 pp. Reprinted 1997 by The Lawbook Exchange, Ltd. LCCN 97-38485. ISBN 1-886363-31-5. Cloth. $75.

Field, Stephen J[ohnson]. *Personal Reminiscences of Early Days in California, with Other Sketches... To Which is added the Story of his Attempted Assassination by a Former Associate on the Supreme Bench of the State by Hon. George C. Gorman.* [Washington, D.C.]: Printed for a Few Friends. Not Published, [1893]. vi, 406 pp. Reprinted 2001 by The Lawbook Exchange, Ltd. LCCN 00-067118. ISBN 1-58477-133-X. Cloth. $85.

Foss, Edward. *A Biographical Dictionary of the Judges of England From the Conquest to the Present Time 1066-1870.* London: John Murray, 1870. xv, 792 pp. Reprinted 2000 by The Lawbook Exchange, Ltd. LCCN 99-12577. ISBN 1-886363-86-2. Cloth. $100.

Goodhart, Arthur L. *Five Jewish Lawyers of the Common Law.* London: Oxford University Press, 1949. [4], 74 pp. Reprinted 2000 by The Lawbook Exchange, Ltd. LCCN 99-049934. ISBN 1-58477-045-7. Cloth. $60.

Hankey, The Right Hon. Lord. *Politics, Trials and Errors.* Chicago: Henry Regnery Company, [1950]. Reprint available 2002 by The Lawbook Exchange, Ltd. ISBN 1-58477-228-X. Cloth. $65.

Harris, Virgil M. *Ancient, Curious, and Famous Wills.* Boston: Little, Brown, and Company, 1911. xiv, 472 pp. Reprinted 1999 by The Lawbook Exchange, Ltd. LCCN 99-20588. ISBN 1-886363-93-5. Cloth. $75.

Hicks, Frederick. *Men and Books Famous in the Law. With an introduction by Harlan F. Stone.* Rochester, New York: Lawyers Co-operative Publishing, 1921. 259 pp. Reprinted 1992 by The Lawbook Exchange, Ltd. LCCN 92-070809. ISBN 0-9630106-2-X. Cloth. $50.

Holdsworth, W.S. *The Historians of Anglo-American Law.* New York: Columbia University Press, 1928. 175 pp. Reprinted 1994 by The Lawbook Exchange, Ltd. ISBN 0-9630106-9-7. Cloth. $50.

Horton, John Theodore. *James Kent: A Study in Conservatism, 1763-1847.* New York: D. Appleton-Century Co., [1939]. xi, 354 pp. Reprinted 2000 by The Lawbook Exchange, Ltd. LCCN 99-056927. ISBN 1-58477-069-4. Cloth. $80.

Jacobs, Clyde E. *Law Writers and the Courts. The Influence of Thomas M. Cooley, Christopher G. Tiedeman, and John F. Dillon upon American Constitutional Law.* Berkeley: University of California Press, 1954. x, 223 pp. Reprinted 2001 by The Lawbook Exchange, Ltd. ISBN 1-58477-195-X. Cloth. $85.

James I. *The Political Works of James I.* Reprinted from the Edition of 1616. With an Introduction by Charles Howard McIlwain. Cambridge: Harvard University Press, 1918. cxi, 354 pp. Reprint available 2002 by The Lawbook Exchange, Ltd. LCCN 2001053981. ISBN 1-58477-222-0. Cloth. $95.

Keasbey, Edward Quinton. *The Courts and Lawyers of New Jersey. 1661-1912.* New York: Lewis Historical Publishing Company, 1912. Three volumes. Illustrated. Reprint available 2002 by The Lawbook Exchange, Ltd. ISBN 1-58477-233-6. Cloth. $295.

Kent, William. *Memoirs and Letters of James Kent, L.L.D.* Boston: Little, Brown, and Company, 1898. x, 341 pp. Reprinted 2001 by The Lawbook Exchange, Ltd. LCCN 00-026688. ISBN 1-58477-100-3. Cloth. $75.

Kilbourn, Dwight C. *The Bench and Bar of Litchfield County, Connecticut 1709-1909: Biographical Sketches of Members. History and Catalogue of the Litchfield Law School. Historical Notes.* Litchfield, Conn.: Published by the Author, 1909. xiv, 344, [3], viii pp.

Illustrated. Reprint available 2002 by The Lawbook Exchange, Ltd. LCCN 2001038974. ISBN 1-58477-213-1. Cloth. $80.

Lansing, John, Jr. *The Delegate from New York or Proceedings of the Federal Convention of 1787 from the Notes of John Lansing, Jr.* Edited by Joseph Reese Strayer. Princeton: Princeton University Press, 1939. x, 125 pp. Reprint available 2002 by The Lawbook Exchange, Ltd. LCCN 2001050456. ISBN 1-58477-218-2. Cloth. $60.

[MacDonell, Sir John and Edward Manson]. *Great Jurists of the World.* Edited by Sir John MacDonell and Edward Manson. With an Introduction by Van Vechten Veeder. Boston: Little, Brown, and Company, 1914. Illustrated. xxxii, 607 pp. Reprinted 1997 by The Lawbook Exchange, Ltd. LCCN 97-8298. ISBN 1-886363-28-5. Cloth. $95.

[Marshall, John]. Servies, James Albert. *A Bibliography of John Marshall.* Washington: United States Commission for the Celebration of the Two Hundredth Anniversary of the Birth of John Marshall, 1956. xix, 182 pp. Reprinted 2000 by The Lawbook Exchange, Ltd. LCCN 99-088239. ISBN 1-58477-083-X. Cloth. $65.

McCulloch, J.R. *The Works of David Ricardo, Esq., M.P. with a Notice of the Life and Writings of the Author.* London: John Murray, 1846. xxxiii, 584 pp. Reprinted 2000 by The Lawbook Exchange, Ltd. LCCN 99-39612. ISBN 1-58477-028-7. Cloth. $90.

[Nichols, J.]. *A Collection of all the Wills, Now Known to Be Extant, of the Kings and Queens of England, Princes and Princesses of Wales, and every Branch of the Blood Royal, from the Reign of William the Conqueror, to that of Henry the Seventh Exclusive: With Explanatory Notes and a Glossary.* London: J. Nichols, 1780. x, 434 pp. Reprinted 1999 by The Lawbook Exchange, Ltd. LCCN 99-17114. ISBN 1-886363-87-0. Cloth. $75.

Oldroyd, Osborn H. *The Assassination of Abraham Lincoln. The Flight, Pursuit, Capture and Punishment of the Conspirators.* Washington, D.C.: O.H. Oldroyd, 1901. xviii, 305pp. Illustrated. Reprint available 2002 by The Lawbook Exchange, Ltd. ISBN 1-58477-125-9. Cloth. $75.

Richards, John T. *Abraham Lincoln The Lawyer-Statesman.* Boston: Houghton Mifflin, 1916. Frontis. Illustrated. xii, 260 pp. Reprinted 1999 by The Lawbook Exchange, Ltd. LCCN 99-20587. ISBN 1-886363-94-3. Cloth. $60.

[Story, Joseph]. Story, William. *Life and Letters of Joseph Story, Associate Justice of the Supreme Court of the United States and Dane Professor of Law at Harvard University, edited by his son, William W. Story.*

Boston: Charles C. Little and James Brown, 1851. Two volumes. xii, 574; viii, 676 pp. Frontispiece. Reprinted 2001 by The Lawbook Exchange, Ltd. LCCN 99-058777. ISBN 1-58477-071-6. Cloth. $195.

[Story, Joseph]. Story, William W., ed. *The Miscellaneous Writings of Joseph Story, Associate Justice of the Supreme Court of the United States and Dane Professor of Law at Harvard University, edited by his son, William W. Story.* Boston: C.C. Little and J. Brown , 1852. x, 828 pp. Reprinted 2001 by The Lawbook Exchange, Ltd. LCCN 99-058559. ISBN 1-58477-072-4. Cloth. $125.

Townsend, William H. *Lincoln the Litigant.* Boston: Houghton Mifflin Company, 1925. [ix], [117] pp. Frontis. Illus. Reprinted 2000 by The Lawbook Exchange, Ltd. LCCN 99-16499. ISBN 1-58477-021-X. Cloth. $60.

Whitney, Henry C. *Life on the Circuit with Lincoln. With Sketches of Generals Grant, Sherman and McClellan, Judge Davis, Leonard Swett, and Other Contemporaries.* Illustrated. Boston: Estes & Lauriat, 1892. viii, 601 pp. Reprinted 2001 by The Lawbook Exchange, Ltd. ISBN 1-58477-115-1. Cloth. $110.

Woolrych, Humphry William. *Lives of Eminent Serjeants-at-Law of the English Bar.* London: Wm. H. Allen & Co., 1869. Two volumes. Reprint available 2002 by The Lawbook Exchange, Ltd. LCCN 2001050455. ISBN 1-58477-217-4. Cloth. $175.

LEGAL CODES

[Field Codes]. [New York 1850-1865]. New York Field Codes. 1850-1865.
Vol. I. *The Code of Civil Procedure of the State of New-York, Reported Complete by the Commissioners on Practice and Pleadings. 1850.*
Vol. II. *The Code of Criminal Procedure of the State of New York, Reported Complete by the Commissioners on Practice and Pleadings. 1850.*
Vol. III. *The Civil Code of the State of New York, Reported Complete by the Commissioners of the Code. 1865.*
Vol. IV. *The Penal Code of the State of New York, Reported Complete by the Commissioners of the Code. 1865.*
Vol. V. *The Political Code of the State of New York. 1860.*
With a new introduction by Michael Weber. Reprinted 1998 by The Lawbook Exchange, Ltd. Five volume series. [8], xcvi, 791; liii, [1], 486; cxii, 776; lxiv, 406, clxvii; xlvii, 607 pp. ISBN 1-886363-40-4 (set). Cloth. $495.

Harper, Robert Francis. *The Code of Hammurabi King of Babylon. About 2250 B.C. Autographed Text transliteration...* Chicago: The

University of Chicago Press, 1904. xxviii, 194, ciii (plates) pp. Illus. Reprinted 2000 The Lawbook Exchange, Ltd. LCCN 99-23953. ISBN 1-58477-003-1. Cloth. $75.

Johns, C.H.W. , translator. *The Oldest Code of Laws in the World: The Code of Laws Promulgated by Hammurabi, King of Babylon, B.C. 2285-2242.* Edinburgh: T. & T. Clark, 1926. xii, 88 pp. Reprinted 2000 by The Lawbook Exchange, Ltd. LCCN 99-053070. ISBN 1-58477-061-9. Cloth. $60.

Livingston, Edward. *A System of Penal Law, for the State of Louisiana: Consisting of A Code of Crimes and Punishments, A Code of Procedure, A Code of Evidence, A Code of Reform and Prison Discipline, A Book of Definitions. Prepared Under the Authority of a Law of the Said State. To Which are Prefixed a Preliminary Report on the Plan of a Penal Code, and Introductory Reports to the Several Codes Embraced in the System of Penal Law.* Philadelphia: James Kay, Jun. & Brother, 1833.v, 745 pp. Reprinted 1999 by The Lawbook Exchange, Ltd. LCCN 99-11403. ISBN 1-886363-83-8. Cloth. $95.

[Macaulay, Thomas Babington]. *A Penal Code Prepared by the Indian Law Commissioners, and published by Command of the Governor General of India in Council.* London: Pelham Richardson, Cornhill, 1838. viii, 138 pp. Reprint available 2002 by The Lawbook Exchange, Ltd. LCCN 99-16486. ISBN 1-58477-018-X. Cloth. $65.

Pharr, Clyde. *The Theodosian Code and Novels and the Sirmondian Constitutions. A Translation with Commentary, Glossary, and Bibliography.* [Princeton]: Princeton University Press, 1952. Quarto. Book measures 9"x12." xxvi, 643pp. Reprinted 2001 by The Lawbook Exchange, Ltd. ISBN 1-58477-146-1. Cloth. $150.

Savigny, Frederick Charles von. *Of the Vocation of Our Age for Legislation and Jurisprudence.* Translated by Abraham Hayward. London: Littlewood, [1831]. ix, [9]-192 pp. Reprint available 2002 by The Lawbook Exchange, Ltd. LCCN 2001041396. ISBN 1-58477-189-5. Cloth. $65.

Schwartz, Bernard, editor. *The Code Napoleon and the Common-Law World. The Sesquicentennial Lectures Delivered at The Law Center of New York University December 13-15, 1954.* New York: New York University Press, 1956. x, 438pp. Reprinted 1998 by The Lawbook Exchange, Ltd. LCCN 98-34100. ISBN 1-886363-59-5. Cloth. $65.

LAW DICTIONARIES, MAXIMS AND QUOTATIONS

Anderson, William C. *A Dictionary of Law, Consisting of Judicial Definitions and Explanations of Words, Phrases, and Maxims, and an Exposition of the Principles of Law: Comprising a Dictionary and Compendium of American and English Jurisprudence.* Chicago: T.H. Flood and Company, 1889. viii, 1140pp. Reprinted 1996 by The Lawbook Exchange, Ltd. LCCN 96-35844. ISBN 1-886363-23-4. Cloth. $125.

Black, Henry Campbell. *A Dictionary of Law. Containing Definitions of the Terms and Phrases of American and English Jurisprudence, Ancient and Modern. Including the Principal Terms of International, Constitutional, and Commercial Law; with a Collection of Legal Maxims and Numerous Select Titles from the Civil Law and Other Foreign Systems.* St. Paul, Minn.: West Publishing, 1891. x, 1253 pp. Reprinted 1991 by the Lawbook Exchange, Ltd. LCCN 91-62383. ISBN 0-9630106-0-3. $150.

Black, Henry Campbell. *A Law Dictionary. Containing Definitions of the Terms and Phrases of American and English Jurisprudence, Ancient and Modern. And Including the Principal Terms of International, Constitutional, Ecclesiastical and Commercial Law, and Medical Jurisprudence, with a Collection of Legal Maxims, Numerous Select Titles from the Roman, Modern Civil, Scotch, French, Spanish, and Mexican Law, and Other Foreign Systems, and a Table of Abbreviations.* St. Paul, Minn.: West Publishing, 1910. 1314 pp. Reprinted 1995 by the Lawbook Exchange, Ltd. LCCN 97-10320. ISBN 1-886363-10-2. Cloth. $150.

Bouvier, John. *A Law Dictionary Adapted to the Constitution and Laws of the United States of America, and of the Several States of the American Union; with References to the Civil and Other Systems of Foreign Law.* Philadelphia: T. & J.W. Johnson, 1839. Two volumes. 559; 628 pp. Reprinted 1993 by The Lawbook Exchange, Ltd. LCCN 99-047231. ISBN 0-9630106-7-0. Cloth. $130.

Broom, Herbert. *A Selection of Legal Maxims, Classified and Illustrated. Eighth American, from the Fifth London Edition, with References to American Cases.* Philadelphia: T. & J.W. Johnson & Co., 1882. lxxviii, 993 [i.e. 779] pp. Reprinted 2000 by The Lawbook Exchange, Ltd. LCCN 99-049329. ISBN 1-58477-052-X. Cloth. $125.

Burrill, Alexander M. *A New Law Dictionary and Glossary: Containing Full Definitions of the Principal Terms of the Common and Civil Law, Together with Translations and Explanations of the Various Technical Phrases in Different Languages, Occurring in the Ancient and Modern Reports, and Standard Treatises; Embracing Also All the Principal Common and Civil Law Maxims. Compiled on the Basis of Spelman's Glossary, and

Adapted to the Jurisprudence of the United States; with Copious Illustrations, Critical and Historical. New York: John S. Voorhies, 1850. Two volumes. xviii, 1099 pp. Reprinted 1998 by The Lawbook Exchange, Ltd. LCCN 97-38481. ISBN 1-886363-32-3. Cloth. $195.

Holthouse, Henry James. *A New Law Dictionary, Containing Explanations of Such Technical Terms and Phrases As Defined in the Works of Legal Authors, in the Practice of the Courts, and in the Parliamentary Proceedings of the Houses of Lords and Commons, To Which Is Added An Outline of An Action at Law and of A Suit in Equity. Edited, from the Second and Enlarged London Edition, With Numerous Additions, by Henry Penington.* Philadelphia: Lea and Blanchard, 1847. viii, [17]-495 pp. Reprinted 1999 by The Lawbook Exchange, Ltd. LCCN 98-49350. ISBN 1-886363-67-6. Cloth. $75.

Jackson, E. Hilton. *Latin for Lawyers. Containing I: A Course in Latin, with Legal Maxims and Phrases As a Basis of Instruction. II. A Collection of Over One Thousand Latin Maxims, with English Translations, Explanatory Notes, and Cross-References. III. A Vocabulary of Latin Words.* London: Sweet & Maxwell, 1915. viii, 300 pp. Reprinted 1992 by The Lawbook Exchange, Ltd. LCCN 92-074408. ISBN 0-9630106-4-6. Cloth. $50.

Jacob, Giles. *The Law-Dictionary: Explaining the Rise, Progress, and Present State of the English Law; Defining and Interpreting the Terms or Words of Art; and Comprising Copious Information on the Subjects of Law, Trade, and Government. Corrected and Greatly Enlarged by T[homas] E[dlyne] Tomlins.* New York: Printed for, and Published by I. Riley, 1811. Six volumes. viii, 531; [2], 543; [2],618; [2], 472; [2], 553; [2], 471pp. Reprinted 2000 by The Lawbook Exchange, Ltd. LCCN 98-49349. ISBN 1-886363-68-4. Cloth. $495.

McNamara, M. Frances. *Ragbag of Legal Quotations.* Albany: Matthew Bender & Company, 1960. xi, 334 pp. Reprinted 1992 by The Lawbook Exchange, Ltd. LCCN 92-074141. ISBN 0-9630106-3-8. Cloth. $50.

Rapalje, Stewart and Lawrence, Robert L. *A Dictionary of American and English Law with Definitions of the Technical Terms of the Canon and Civil Laws. Also, Containing a Full Collection of Latin Maxims, and Citations of Upwards of Forty Thousand Reported Cases, in which Words and Phrases Have Been Judicially Defined or Construed.* Jersey City: Frederick C. Linn & Co., 1888. Two volumes. xxxviii, 1380 pp. Reprinted 1997 by The Lawbook Exchange, Ltd. LCCN 97-38484. ISBN 1-886363-33-1. Cloth. $195.

Shumaker, Walter A. *The Cyclopedic Law Dictionary Comprising the Terms and Phrases of American Jurisprudence, Including Ancient and*

Modern Common Law, International Law, and Numerous Select Titles from the Civil Law, the French and the Spanish Law, etc., etc. with an Exhaustive Collection of Legal Maxims. Second Edition by James C. Cahill. Chicago: Callaghan and Company, 1922. xii, 545 pp. Reprinted 2001 by The Lawbook Exchange, Ltd. LCCN 99-11404. ISBN 1-886363-85-4. Cloth. $150.

Stimson, Frederic Jesup. *Glossary of Technical Terms, Phrases, and Maxims of the Common Law.* Boston: Little, Brown, and Company, 1881. iv, 305pp. Reprinted 1999 by The Lawbook Exchange, Ltd. LCCN 98-50813. ISBN 1-886363-70-6. Cloth. $60.

Trayner, John. *Latin Phrases and Maxims: Collected from the Institutional and other Writers on Scotch Law; with Translations and Illustrations.* Edinburgh: William Paterson, 1861. iv, [2], 356 pp. Reprinted 2001 by The Lawbook Exchange, Ltd. LCCN 00-067012. ISBN 1-58477-174-7. Cloth. $75.

LEGAL HISTORY

Adams, W.H. Davenport. *Learned in the Law; or Examples and Encouragements from the Lives of Eminent Lawyers.* London: S.W. Partridge & Co., [1882?]. vi, 392 pp. Reprint available 2002 by The Lawbook Exchange, Ltd. ISBN 1-58477-238-7. Cloth. $80.

Anthony, Susan B. *An Account of the Proceedings of the Trial of Susan B. Anthony, on the Charge of Illegal Voting, at the Presidential Election in Nov., 1872. and on the Trial of Beverly W. Jones, Edwin T. Marsh and William B. Hall, the Inspectors of Election by whom her Vote was Received.* Rochester: Daily Democrat and Chronicle Book Print, 1874. vii, 212 pp. Reprint available 2002 by The Lawbook Exchange, Ltd. LCCN 2001041397. ISBN 1-58477-187-9. Cloth. $65.

Bar, Carl Ludwig von. *A History of Continental Criminal Law.* Boston: Little, Brown, and Company, 1916. lvi, 561 pp. Reprinted 1999 by The Lawbook Exchange, Ltd. LCCN 99-32341. ISBN 1-58477-013-9. Cloth. $90.

Beard, Charles Austin. *The Office of the Justice of the Peace in England, in its Origin and Development.* New York: Columbia University Press, 1904. 184, [1] pp. Reprinted 2001 by The Lawbook Exchange, Ltd. ISBN 1-58477-102-X. Cloth. $60.

Bouvier, John. *Institutes of American Law. New Edition by Daniel A. Gleason. In Two Volumes.* Boston: Little, Brown, & Company, 1880. lxviii, 651; iv, 798 pp. Reprinted 1999 by The Lawbook Exchange,

Ltd. LCCN 98-54288. ISBN 1-886363-80-3. Cloth. $250.

Cawston, George and A.H. Keane. *The Early Chartered Companies (A.D. 1296-1858)*. London: Edward Arnold, 1896. Frontispiece. xi, 329 pp. Reprint available 2002 by The Lawbook Exchange, Ltd. LCCN 2001041393. ISBN 1-58477-196-8. Cloth. $75.

[Cherokee Laws]. *Compiled Laws of the Cherokee Nation.* Tahlequah, I.T.:National Advocate Print, 1881. 370pp. Reprinted September 1998 by The Lawbook Exchange, Ltd. With a new introduction by Michael Weber. LCCN 98-12741. ISBN 1-886363-42-0. Cloth. $60.

Cherry, Richard R. *Lectures on the Growth of Criminal Law in Ancient Communities.* London: Macmillan and Co., 1890. xi, 123 pp. Reprinted 2002 by The Lawbook Exchange, Ltd. LCCN 00-067010. ISBN 1-58477-167-4. Cloth. $65.

Chitwood, Oliver Perry. *Justice in Colonial Virginia.* Baltimore: Johns Hopkins Press, 1905. 123, [1] pp. Reprinted 2001 by The Lawbook Exchange, Ltd. ISBN 1-58477-114-3. Cloth. $65.

Coke, Edward Sir. *The First Part of the Institute of the Laws of England, or, A commentary upon Littleton. Not the name of the Author only, but of the Law Itself. Revised and Corrected With Additions of Notes, References, and Proper Tables, by Francis Hargrave and Charles Butler, Esqrs. Of Lincoln's Inn, Including also The Notes of Lord Chief Justice Hale and Lord Chancellor Nottingham; and An Analysis of Littleton, written by an unknown Hand in 1658-9.* By Charles Butler, Esq. The Eighteenth Edition, Corrected. London, J. & W.T. Clarke, 1823. Two volumes. ccxvi,[606]; iv, [772] pp. Reprinted 2000 by The Lawbook Exchange, Ltd. LCCN 99-41675. ISBN 1-58477-033-3. Cloth. $195.

Coke, Sir Edward. *The Second Part of the Institutes of the Laws of England; Containing the Exposition of Many Ancient and Other Statutes.* London: Printed for W. Clarke and Sons, 1817. Star-paged. [18], 746, [49] pp. Reprinted 2002 by The Lawbook Exchange, Ltd. ISBN 1-58477-200-X. Cloth. $125.

Coke, Sir Edward. *The Third Part of the Institutes of the Laws of England; Concerning High Treason, and Other Pleas of the Crown and Criminal Causes.* London: Printed for W. Clarke and Sons, 1817. Star-paged. [10], [244], [20] pp. Reprinted 2002 by The Lawbook Exchange, Ltd. ISBN 1-58477-201-8. Cloth. $75.

Coke, Sir Edward. *The Fourth Part of the Institutes of the Laws of England; Concerning The Jurisdiction of the Courts.* London: Printed for W. Clarke and Sons, 1817. Star-paged. [12], 364, [49] pp.

Reprinted 2002 by The Lawbook Exchange, Ltd. ISBN 1-58477-202-6. Cloth. $85.

Coke, Sir Edward. *The Reports of Sir Edward Coke, Knt. In Thirteen Parts. A New Edition, with Additional Notes and References, and with Abstracts of the Principal Points: The First Three Parts and the Fourth to Fol. 38a. by John Henry Thomas, Esq. The Rest of the Fourth and the Remaining Nine Parts by John Farquhar Fraser, Esq.* Boston: Little Brown, and Company, 1826. Six volumes. With a new introduction by Stephen M. Sheppard. Reprint available 2002 by The Lawbook Exchange, Ltd. ISBN 1-58477-239-5. Cloth. $595.

[Continental Legal History]. *A General Survey of Events, Sources, Persons & Movements in Continental Legal History. By Various European Authors.* With an introduction by Albert Kocourek. Boston: Little, Brown, 1912. liii, 754pp. Reprinted 1998 by The Lawbook Exchange, Ltd. LCCN 98-11159. ISBN 1-886363-47-1. Cloth. $110.

Darrow, Clarence and William J. Bryan. *The World's Most Famous Court Trial. Tennessee Evolution Case. A Complete Stenographic Report of the Famous Court Test of the Anti-Evolution Act, at Dayton July 10 to 21, 1925, Including Speeches and Arguments of Attorneys.* Cincinnati: National Book Company, [1925]. [4], 339 pp. Reprinted 1997 by The Lawbook Exchange, Ltd. LCCN 97-38485. ISBN 1-886363-31-5. Cloth. $75.

Dawson, John P. *A History of Lay Judges.* Cambridge, Mass.: Harvard University Press, 1960. viii, [2], 310 pp. Reprinted 1999 by The Lawbook Exchange, Ltd. LCCN 98-50812. ISBN 1-886363-69-2. Cloth. $75.

Dodd, Walter Fairleigh. *The Revision and Amendment of State Constitutions.* Baltimore: The Johns Hopkins Press, 1910. xvii, 350 pp. Reprinted 1999 by The Lawbook Exchange, Ltd. LCCN 98-50815. ISBN 1-886363-73-0. Cloth. $65.

Esmein, A[dhemar]. *A History of Continental Criminal Procedure with Special Reference to France. Translated by John Simpson; with an editorial preface by William E. Mikell and introductions by Norman M. Trenholme and by William Renwick Riddell.* Boston: Little, Brown and Company, 1913. xlv, 640 pp. Reprinted 2000 by The Lawbook Exchange, Ltd. LCCN 99-045906. ISBN 1-58477-042-2. Cloth. $100.

Evans, E.P. *The Criminal Prosecution and Capital Punishment of Animals.* New York: E.P. Dutton, 1906. x, 384pp. Reprinted 1998 by The Lawbook Exchange, Ltd. LCCN 98-12801. ISBN 1-886363-52-8. Cloth. $65.

Farnam, Henry W. *Chapters in the History of Social Legislation in the United States to 1860.* Washington: Carnegie Institution of Washington, 1938. xx, 496 pp. Reprinted 2000 by The Lawbook Exchange, Ltd. LCCN 99-049362. ISBN 1-58477-054-6. Cloth. $100.

Forsyth, William. *The History of Lawyers. Ancient and Modern.* Boston: Estes & Lauriat, 1875. Illustrated. xvii, 404 pp. Reprinted 1996 by the Lawbook Exchange, Ltd. LCCN 95-51103. ISBN 1-886363-14-5. Cloth. $60.

Forsyth, William. *History of Trial by Jury* [*Second edition*]. Jersey City: Frederick D. Linn, [1875]. x, 388 pp. Reprinted 1994 by The Lawbook Exchange, Ltd. LCCN 96-14505. ISBN 0-9630106-8-9. Cloth. $65.

Fortescue, Sir John. *DeLaudibus Legum Angliae. A Treatise in Commendation of the Laws of England.* With Translation by Francis Gregor. Notes by Andrew Amos and a Life of the Author by Thomas (Fortescue) Lord Clermont. Cincinnati: Robert Clarke & Co., 1874. lxiv, 302 pp. Reprinted 1999 by The Lawbook Exchange, Ltd. LCCN 99-16485. ISBN 1-58477-019-8. Cloth. $65.

Fortescue, Sir John. *The Governance of England: Otherwise Called The Difference between an Absolute and a Limited Monarchy. A Revised Text edited with Introduction, Notes, and Appendices by Charles Plummer.* London: Oxford University Press, 1885. xxiii, 387pp. Reprinted 1999 by The Lawbook Exchange, Ltd. ISBN 1-886363-79-X. Cloth. $65.

Futrell, William H. *The History of American Customs Jurisprudence.* New York: Published privately, 1941. 314pp. Reprinted 1998 by The Lawbook Exchange, Ltd. LCCN 98-11342. ISBN 1-886363-51-X. Cloth. $60.

Gierke, Otto. *Political Theories of the Middle Ages.* Translated with an introduction by Frederick William Maitland. Cambridge: At the University Press, 1913. lxxx, 197 pp. Reprinted 2002 by The Lawbook Exchange, Ltd. LCCN 2001041398. ISBN 1-58477-186-0. Cloth. $70.

Giesecke, Albert Anthony. *American Commercial Legislation Before 1789.* New York: University of Pennsylvania: D. Appleton and Company, agents, 1910. 167 pp. Reprinted 2001 by The Lawbook Exchange, Ltd. LCCN 00-058813. ISBN 1-58477-153-4. Cloth. $65.

Haines, Charles Grove. *The Conflict over Judicial Powers in the United States to 1870.* New York: Columbia University Press, 1909.

180 pp. Reprinted 2001 by The Lawbook Exchange, Ltd. LCCN 99-088241. ISBN 1-58477-080-5. Cloth. $60.

Hale, Matthew. *The History and Analysis of the Common Law of England.* Stafford: J. Nutt, 1713. [x], 264, [28], 176 pp. Reprinted 2000 by The Lawbook Exchange, Ltd. LCCN 99-33739. ISBN 1-58477-024-4. Cloth. $85.

Hankey, The Right Hon. Lord. *Politics, Trials and Errors.* Chicago: Henry Regnery Company, [1950]. Reprint available 2002 by The Lawbook Exchange, Ltd. ISBN 1-58477-228-X. Cloth. $65.

Hearn, William Edward. *The Aryan Household Its Structure and its Development. An Introduction to Comparative Jurisprudence.* London and New York: Longmans, Green, and Co., 1891. viii, 494 pp. Reprint available 2002 by The Lawbook Exchange, Ltd. ISBN 1-58477-124-0. Cloth. $90.

Hepburn, Charles M. *The Historical Development of Code Pleading in America and England with Special Reference to the Codes of New York, Missouri, California, Kentucky, Iowa, Minnesota, Indiana, Ohio, Oregon, Washington, Nebraska, Wisconsin, Kansas, Nevada, North Dakota, South Dakota, Idaho, Montana, Arizona, North Carolina, South Carolina, Arkansas, Wyoming, Utah, Colorado, Connecticut, and Oklahoma.* Cincinnati: W.H. Anderson & Co., 1897. xvi, 318 pp. Reprint available 2002 by The Lawbook Exchange, Ltd. LCCN 2001050458. ISBN 1-58477-220-4. Cloth. $75.

Holdsworth, William S. *Essays in Law and History.* Edited by A.L. Goodhart and H.G. Hanbury. Oxford: At the Clarendon Press, 1946. xv, 302 pp. Reprinted 1995 by The Lawbook Exchange, Ltd. LCCN 99-047234. ISBN 1-886363-13-7. Cloth. $65.

Holt, W. Stull. *Treaties Defeated by the Senate. A Study of the Struggle Between President and Senate Over the Conduct of Foreign Relations.* Baltimore: The Johns Hopkins Press, 1933. vi, [1],328 pp. Reprinted 2000 by The Lawbook Exchange, Ltd. LCCN 99-39606. ISBN 1-58477-029-5. Cloth. $65.

Hurst, James Willard. *The Growth of American Law: The Law Makers.* Boston: Little, Brown and Company, 1950. xiii, 502 pp. Reprinted 2001 by The Lawbook Exchange, Ltd. ISBN 1-58477-194-1. Cloth. $90.

Hurst, James Willard. *Law and Social Order in the United States.* Ithaca: Cornell University Press, 1977. 318 pp. Reprinted 2000 by The Lawbook Exchange, Ltd. ISBN 1-58477-113-5. Cloth. $85.

Ilbert, Courtenay. *The Mechanics of Law Making.* New York: Columbia University Press, 1914. viii, 209 pp. Reprinted 2001 by The Lawbook Exchange, Ltd. LCCN 99-047156. ISBN 1-58477-044-9. Cloth. $70.

James I. *The Political Works of James I.* Reprinted from the Edition of 1616. With an Introduction by Charles Howard McIlwain. Cambridge: Harvard University Press, 1918. cxi, 354 pp. Reprint available 2002 by The Lawbook Exchange, Ltd. LCCN 2001053981. ISBN 1-58477-222-0. Cloth. $95.

Jenks, Edward. *The Constitutional Experiments of the Commonwealth: A Study of the Years 1649-1660.* Cambridge: The University Press, 1890. iv, 154 pp. Reprint available 2002 by The Lawbook Exchange, Ltd. LCCN 00-067823. ISBN 1-58477-141-0. Cloth. $60.

Johnson, Hebert Alan. *The Law Merchant and Negotiable Instruments in Colonial New York, 1664 to 1730.* Chicago: Loyola University Press, 1963. Reprint available 2002 by The Lawbook Exchange, Ltd. LCCN 2001037701. ISBN 1-58477-208-5. Cloth. $60.

Kames, Henry Home, Lord. *Historical Law-Tracts. The Second Edition.* Edinburgh: A. Kincaid, 1761. xv, 463 pp. LCCN 99-43133. ISBN 1-58477-038-4. Reprinted 2000 by The Lawbook Exchange, Ltd. Cloth. $95.

Keller, Morton. *Affairs of State: Public Life in Late Nineteenth Century America.* Cambridge: Harvard University Press, 1977. ix, 631 pp. Reprinted 2000 by The Lawbook Exchange, Ltd. LCCN 99-087921. ISBN 1-58477-086-4. Cloth. $95.

Kitchin, S.B. *A History of Divorce.* London: Chapman & Hall, Ltd., 1912. xvi, 293 pp. Reprint available 2002 by The Lawbook Exchange, Ltd. LCCN 2001041400. ISBN 1-58477-190-9. Cloth. $75.

Leaming, Aaron and Jacob Spicer. *The Grants, Concessions, and Original Constitutions of the Province of New Jersey: The Acts Passed during the Proprietary Governments, and other material Transactions before the Surrender thereof to Queen Anne The Instrument of Surrender, and her formal Acceptance thereof, Lord Cornbury's Commission and Instructions Consequent thereon, Collected by some Gentlemen employed by the General Assembly. And afterwards Published by virtue of an Act of the Legislature of the said Province With proper Tables alphabetically Digested, containing the principal Matters in the Book.* Philadelphia: W. Bradford, [1881]. [vi], 763 pp. Reprint available 2002 by The Lawbook Exchange, Ltd. LCCN 2001050457. ISBN 1-58477-219-0. Cloth. $135.

[Legal History]. *Select Essays in Anglo-American Legal History. By Maitland, Pollock, Holmes, Beale, Holdsworth and Others.* Boston: Little, Brown, and Company, 1907. Three volumes. 847; 823; 862 pp. Reprinted 1992 by The Lawbook Exchange, Ltd. LCCN 91-77977. ISBN 0-9630106-1-1. Cloth. $195.

Maitland, Frederick W., Montague, Francis C., *A Sketch of English Legal History.* Edited with Notes and Appendices by James F. Colby. New York: G.P. Putnam's Sons, 1915. x, 234pp. Reprinted 1998 by The Lawbook Exchange, Ltd. LCCN 98-11337. ISBN 1-886363-50-1. Cloth. $50.

Maitland, Frederick William. *English Law and the Renaissance (The Rede Lecture for 1901) with Some Notes.* Cambridge: at the University Press, 1901. 98 pp. Reprinted 2000 by The Lawbook Exchange, Ltd. LCCN 99-41654. ISBN 1-58477-034-1. Cloth. $60.

Maitland, F.W. *The Constitutional History of England. A Course of Lectures Delivered.* Cambridge: Cambridge University Press, 1908. xxviii, 547 pp. Reprinted 2001 by The Lawbook Exchange, Ltd. LCCN 00-068895. ISBN 1-58477-148-8. Cloth. $95.

McKechnie, William Sharp. *Magna Carta. A Commentary on the Great Charter of King John. With an Historical Introduction. Second Edition, Revised and in part Re-written.* Glasgow: James Maclehose and Sons, 1914. xvii,530, [2] pp. Reprinted 2000 by The Lawbook Exchange, Ltd. LCCN 99-38731. ISBN 1-58477-031-7. Cloth. $95.

Merriam, C.E., Jr. *History of the Theory of Sovereignty Since Rousseau.* New York: Columbia University Press, [1900]. x, [11]-233 pp. Reprinted 1999 by The Lawbook Exchange, Ltd. LCCN 98-32385. ISBN 1-886363-76-5. Cloth. $65.

Morris, Thomas D. *Free Men All: The Personal Liberty Laws of the North 1780-1861.* Baltimore: The Johns Hopkins University Press, 1974. xii, 253 pp. Reprinted 2001 by The Lawbook Exchange, Ltd. ISBN 1-58477-107-0. Cloth. $75.

Neilson, George. *Trial by Combat.* Glasgow: William Hodge & Co., 1890. xiv, 348 pp. Reprinted 2000 by The Lawbook Exchange, Ltd. LCCN 99-059101. ISBN 1-58477-075-9. Cloth. $75.

[Parker, James]. [Legal Manual]. *Conductor Generalis, or The Office, Duty and Authority of Justices of the Peace, High Sheriffs, Under-Sheriffs, Goalers, Coroners, Constables, Jury Men, Over-seers of the Poor, and also The Office of Clerks of Assiza And of the Peace &c. Collected out of all the Books hitherto written on those Subjects, whether of Common or Statute Law. To which is added, A Collection out of Sir Matthew Hales* *concerning The Descent of Lands. The Whole Alphabetically Digested Under the Several Titles, With a Table Directing to the Ready finding out Proper Matter under those Titles.* Philadelphia: Printed and Sold by Andrew Bradford, 1722. [8], xii, 232pp. **[with]** *The Office, Duty and Authority of Sheriffs, How and in what Manner to execute the same, according to the Common and Statute Laws of Great-Britain, which are now in Force and Use. Likewise, Of Under-Sheriffs and their Deputies; and where the High-Sheriff shall be answerable for their Defaults, and where not, &c.* Philadelphia: Andrew Bradford, 1721. [233]-299, [1] pp. Reprint available 2002 by The Lawbook Exchange, Ltd. LCCN 00-058810. ISBN 1-58477-123-2. Cloth. $80.

Perry, Ross R. *Common-law Pleading: Its History and Principles. Including Dicey's Rules Concerning Parties to Action and Stephen's Rules of Pleading.* Boston, Little, Brown and Company, 1897. xxvi, 494 pp. Reprinted 2001 by The Lawbook Exchange, Ltd. ISBN 1-58477-105-4. Cloth. $95.

Plucknett, Theodore F.T. *A Concise History of the Common Law. Fifth Edition.* Boston: Little, Brown and Company, 1956. Reprinted 2001 by The Lawbook Exchange, Ltd. LCCN 00-067821. ISBN 1-58477-137-2. Cloth. $125.

Powell, Chilton Latham. *English Domestic Relations 1487-1653. A Study of Matrimony and Family Life in Theory and Practice as Revealed by the Literature, Law, and History of the Period.* New York: Columbia University Press, 1917. xii, 274 pp. Reprinted 2001 by The Lawbook Exchange, Ltd. ISBN 1-58477-096-1. Cloth. $75.

Schechter, Frank I. *The Historical Foundations of the Law Relating to Trade-Marks.* New York: Columbia University Press, 1925. xxviii, 211 pp. Reprinted 2000 by The Lawbook Exchange, Ltd. LCCN 99-41673. ISBN 1-58477-035-X. Cloth. $60.

Scott, Henry W. *The Courts of the State of New York: Their History, Development and Jurisdiction: Embracing a complete history of all the Courts and Tribunals of Justice, both Colonial and State, established from the first settlement of Manhattan Island and including the status and jurisdiction of all the Courts of the State as now constituted.* New York: Wilson Publishing Co., 1909. iv, 506 pp. Reprinted 2001 by The Lawbook Exchange, Ltd. LCCN 99-10259. ISBN 1-886363-84-6. Cloth. $95.

Stimson, Frederic Jesup. *Popular Law-Making. A Study of the Origin, History, and Present Tendencies of Law-Making by Statute.* New York: Charles Scribner's Sons, 1910. xii, 545 pp. Reprint available 2002 by The Lawbook Exchange, Ltd. LCCN 00-022513. ISBN 1-58477-094-5. Cloth. $85.

Stokes, Anthony. *A View of the Constitution of the British Colonies, in North-America and the West-Indies, at the Time the Civil War Broke Out on the Continent of America.* London: Printed for the author and sold by B. White, 1783. 555, (1) pp. Reprint available 2002 by The Lawbook Exchange, Ltd. LCCN 2001050735. ISBN 1-58477-224-7. Cloth. $90.

Stokes, I.N. Phelps. *The Iconography of Manhattan Island 1498-1909.* New York: Robert H. Dodd, 1915. Six volumes. Reprinted 1998 by The Lawbook Exchange, Ltd. LCCN 97-30604. ISBN 1-886363-30-7. Cloth. $750.

Thomson, Richard. *An Historical Essay on the Magna Charta of King John: to which are added, the Great Charter in Latin and English, the charters of liberties and confirmations, granted by Henry III and Edward I, the original Charter of the forests, and various authentic instruments connected with them: Explanatory Notes on their Several Privileges; A Descriptive Account of the Principal Originals and Editions Extant, Both in Print and Manuscript; and Other Illustrations, Derived from the Most Interesting and Authentic Sources.* London: John Major and Robert Jennings, 1829. xxxii, 612 pp. Reprinted 2000 by The Lawbook Exchange, Ltd. LCCN 99-40987. ISBN 1-58477-030-9. Cloth. $95.

[Trials]. [Witchcraft Trials]. *Curious Cases and Amusing Actions at Law Including Some Trials of Witches in the Seventeenth Century.* Toronto: The Carswell Co., Limited, 1916. vii, 234 pp. Reprinted 2000 by The Lawbook Exchange, Ltd. LCCN 99-032361. ISBN 1-58477-012-0. Cloth. $65.

FREEDOM OF SPEECH

Chafee, Zechariah. *Free Speech in the United States.* Cambridge, Massachusetts: Harvard University Press, 1967. xviii, 634 pp. Reprinted 2001 by The Lawbook Exchange, Ltd. LCCN 99-087317. ISBN 1-58477-085-6. Cloth. $125.

Cooper, Thomas. *A Treatise on the Law of Libel and the Liberty of the Press; Showing the Origin, Use, and Abuse of the Law of Libel: With Copious Notes and References to Authorities in Great Britain and the United States: As Applicable to Individuals and to Political and Ecclesiastical Bodies and Principles.* New York: G.F. Hopkins & Son, 1830. xxxviii, 184 pp. Reprint available 2002 by The Lawbook Exchange, Ltd. ISBN 1-58477-134-8. Cloth. $75.

Meiklejohn, Alexander. *Free Speech and Its Relation to Self Government.* New York: Harper Brothers Publishers, [1948]. xiv,

107pp. Reprinted 2001 by The Lawbook Exchange, Ltd. LCCN 99-87204. ISBN 1-58477-087-2. Cloth. $80.

Schroeder, Theodore. *Constitutional Free Speech Defined and Defended in an Unfinished Argument in a Case of Blasphemy.* New York: Free Speech League, 1919. 456 pp. Reprinted 2001 by The Lawbook Exchange, Ltd. LCCN 99-049361. ISBN 1-58477-053-8. Cloth. $90.

Schroeder, Theodore. *Free Speech Bibliography Including Every Discovered Attitude Toward the Problem Covering Every Method of Transmitting Ideas and Abridging Their Promulgation upon Every Subject-Matter.* New York: The H.W. Wilson Company, 1922. [vii], 247 pp. Reprinted 2001 by The Lawbook Exchange, Ltd. LCCN 99-049361. ISBN 1-58477-053-8. Cloth. $85.

Schroeder, Theodore. *"Obscene" Literature and Constitutional Law. A Forensic Defense of Freedom of the Press.* New York: Privately Printed for Forensic Uses, 1911. 439 pp. Reprint available 2002 by The Lawbook Exchange, Ltd. LCCN 00-58815. ISBN 1-58477-154-2. Cloth. $85.

INTERNATIONAL LAW

Grotius, Hugo. *The Freedom of the Seas or The Right which Belongs to the Dutch to Take Part in the East Indian Trade.* Translated with a Revision of the Latin Text of 1633 by Ralph van Deman Magoffin. Edited with an Introductory Note by James Brown Scott. New York: Oxford University Press, 1916. xv, 83pp., paged in duplicate. Reprinted 2001 by The Lawbook Exchange, Ltd. LCCN 2001022509. ISBN 1-58477-182-8. Cloth. $65.

Huebner, Rudolf. *A History of Germanic Private Law.* Translated by Francis S. Philbrick; with an editorial preface by Ernest G. Lorenzen and introductions by Paul Vinogradoff and by William E. Walz. Boston: Little, Brown and Company, 1818. lix, 788 pp. Reprinted 2000 by The Lawbook Exchange, Ltd. LCCN 99-055138. ISBN 1-58477-065-1. Cloth. $120.

Kelsen, Hans. *Collective Security under International Law.* Washington, D.C.: United States Government Printing Office, 1957. Reprinted 2001 by The Lawbook Exchange, Ltd. LCCN 00-053507. ISBN 1-58477-144-5. Cloth. $70.

Kelsen, Hans. *The Law of the United Nations. A Critical Analysis of Its Fundamental Problems.* New York: Frederick A. Praeger, [1964]. xvii, 994 pp. Reprinted 2000 by The Lawbook Exchange, Ltd. ISBN 1-58477-077-5. Cloth. $125.

Kovalevsky, Maxime. *Modern Customs and Ancient Laws of Russia. Being the Ilchester Lectures for 1889-90.* London: David Nutt, 1891. x, 260 pp. Reprinted 2000 by The Lawbook Exchange, Ltd. LCCN 99-16487. ISBN 1-58477-017-1. Cloth. $65.

Lauterpacht, H[ersch]. *The Function of Law in the International Community.* Oxford: Clarendon Press, 1933. xxvi, 470 pp. Reprinted 2000 by The Lawbook Exchange, Ltd. LCCN 00-022124. ISBN 1-58477-090-2. Cloth. $90.

Lauterpacht, Hersch, Sir. *Private Law Sources and Analogies of International Law: With Special Reference to International Arbitration.* London: Longmans, Green and Co. Ltd., 1927. xxv, 325 pp. Reprint available 2002 by The Lawbook Exchange, Ltd. LCCN 2001041399. ISBN 1-58477-184-4. Cloth. $75.

Morris, Robert C. *International Arbitration and Procedure.* New Haven: Yale University Press, 1911. x, 238 pp. Reprinted 2001 by The Lawbook Exchange, Ltd. LCCN 00-059547. ISBN 1-58477-160-7. Cloth. $70.

Orfield, Lester Bernhardt. *The Growth of Scandinavian Law.* Philadelphia: University of Pennsylvania Press for Temple University Publications, 1953. xx, 363 pp. Reprint available 2002 by The Lawbook Exchange, Ltd. LCCN 2001023454. ISBN 1-58477-180-1. Cloth. $80.

Scott, James Brown. *Law, The State, and the International Community.* New York: Columbia University Press, 1939. Two volumes. Reprint available 2002 by The Lawbook Exchange, Ltd. LCCN 2001018648. ISBN 1-58477-178-X. Cloth. $175.

Scott, James Brown. *The Spanish Origin of International Law. Francisco De Vitoria and His Law of Nations.* London: Humphrey Milford, 1934. 19a, 288, clviii pp. Frontispiece and portrait. Reprinted 2000 by The Lawbook Exchange, Ltd. LCCN 00-036835. ISBN 1-58477-110-0. Cloth. $90.

Wheaton, Henry. *Elements of International Law: with a Sketch of the History of the Science.* Philadelphia: Carey, Lea & Blanchard, 1836. xiv, 375 pp. Reprint available 2002 by The Lawbook Exchange, Ltd. LCCN 00-066335. ISBN 1-58477-170-4. Cloth. $80.

Wiener, Leo. *Commentary to the Germanic Laws and Mediaeval Documents.* Cambridge: Harvard University Press, 1915. lxi, 224 pp. Reprinted 2000 by The Lawbook Exchange, Ltd. LCCN 99-23969. ISBN 1-58477-005-8. Cloth. $60.

Woodbine, George E. *Four Thirteenth Century Law Tracts. A Thesis Presented to the Faculty of the Graduate School of Yale University in Candidacy for the Degree of Doctor of Philosophy.* New Haven: Yale University Press, 1910. vi, 183 pp. Reprinted 1999 by The Lawbook Exchange, Ltd. LCCN 99-29294. ISBN 1-58477-007-4. Cloth. $50.

JURISPRUDENCE AND PHILOSOPHY OF LAW

Austin, John. *The Province of Jurisprudence Determined.* London: John Murray, 1832. xx, 392, lxxvi pp. Reprinted 2000 by The Lawbook Exchange, Ltd. LCCN 99-33457. ISBN 1-58477-023-6. Cloth. $75.

Beck, Theodric Romeyn. *Elements of Medical Jurisprudence.* Albany: Websters and Skinners, 1823. Two volumes. xxxiv, 418; viii, [9]-471 pp. Reprinted 1997 by The Lawbook Exchange, Ltd. LCCN 96-35845. ISBN 1-886363-24-2. Cloth. $125.

Bentham, Jeremy. *A Fragment on Government. Edited with an Introduction by F.C. Montague.* Oxford: The Clarendon Press, 1891. xii, 241 pp. Reprinted 2001 by The Lawbook Exchange, Ltd. ISBN 1-58477-166-6. Cloth. $65.

Bentham, Jeremy. *Plan of Parliamentary Reform, in the Form of a Catechism, with Reasons for each Article. With an Introduction, Shewing the Necessity of Radical, and the Inadequacy of Moderate, Reform.* London: T.J. Wooler, 1818. 156 pp. Reprint available 2002 by The Lawbook Exchange, Ltd. LCCN 00-058816. ISBN 1-58477-121-6. Cloth. $65.

Calabresi, Guido. *A Common Law for the Age of Statutes.* Cambridge: Harvard University Press, 1982. xi, 319 pp. Reprinted 2000 by The Lawbook Exchange, Ltd. LCCN 99-44889. ISBN 1-58477-040-6. Cloth. $85.

Cardozo, Benjamin. *The Paradoxes of Legal Science.* New York: Columbia University Press, 1928. v, 142 pp. Reprinted 2000 by The Lawbook Exchange, Ltd. LCCN 00-024469. ISBN 1-58477-097-X. Cloth. $75.

Davis, Horace A. *The Judicial Veto.* Boston: Houghton Mifflin Company, 1914. vi, 148 pp. Reprint available 2002 by The Lawbook Exchange, Ltd. LCCN 2001045982. ISBN 1-58477-212-3. Cloth. $60.

Emery, Lucilius A. *Concerning Justice.* New Haven: Yale University Press, 1914. Reprint available 2002 by The Lawbook Exchange, Ltd. ISBN 1-58477-234-4. Cloth. $60.

Field, Oliver P. *The Effect of an Unconstitutional Statute.* Minneapolis: University of Minnesota Press, 1935. xi, 355 pp. Reprint available 2002 by The Lawbook Exchange, Ltd. LCCN 2001022508. ISBN 1-58477-181-X. Cloth. $80.

Fuller, Lon L. *The Law in Quest of Itself.* Boston: Beacon Press, 1966. [vi], 150 pp. Reprinted 1999 by The Lawbook Exchange, Ltd. LCCN 99-32863. ISBN 1-58477-016-3. Cloth. $45.

Gierke, Otto. *Natural Law and the Theory of Society 1500 to 1800.* With a Lecture on the Ideas of Natural Law and Humanity by Ernst Troeltsch. Translated with an Introduction by Ernest Barker. Complete in one volume. Cambridge: The University Press, 1950. Reprinted 2001 by The Lawbook Exchange, Ltd. LCCN 2001016483. ISBN 1-58477-149-6. Cloth. $110.

Hohfeld, Wesley. *Fundamental Legal Conceptions as Applied in Judicial Reasoning.*Edited by Walter Wheeler Cook, with a New Foreword by Arthur L. Corbin. New Haven: Yale University Press, 1964. xv, 114 pp. Reprinted 2000 by The Lawbook Exchange, Ltd. LCCN 00-064108. ISBN 1-58477-162-3. Cloth. $55.

Jhering, Rudolf Von. *Law as a Means to an End.* Translated from the German by Isaac Husik with an Editorial Preface by Joseph H. Drake and with Introductions by Henry Lamm and W.M. Geldart. Boston: The Boston Book Company, 1913. lxi, 483 pp. Reprinted 1999 by The Lawbook Exchange, Ltd. LCCN 99-23754. ISBN 1-58477-009-0. Cloth. $80.

Jhering, Rudolph von. *The Struggle for Law. Translated from the Fifth German Edition by John J. Lalor. Second Edition, with an Introduction by Albert Kocourek.* Chicago: Callaghan and Company, 1915. lii, 138 pp. Reprinted 1997 by The Lawbook Exchange, Ltd. LCCN 97-6826. ISBN 1-886363-25-0. Cloth. $60.

Kant, Immanuel. *The Philosophy of Law: An Exposition of the Fundamental Principles of Jurisprudence as the Science of Right.* Translated from the German by W. Hastie, B.D. Edinburgh: T. & T. Clark, 1887. xxxvi, 265 pp. Reprint available 2002 by The Lawbook Exchange, Ltd. LCCN 00-066332. ISBN 1-58477-131-3. Cloth. $70.

Kelsen, Hans. *General Theory of Law and State.* Translated by Anders Wedberg. Cambridge: Harvard University Press, 1945. xxxiii, 516pp. Reprinted 1999 by The Lawbook Exchange, Ltd. LCCN 98-32334. ISBN 1-886363-74-9. Cloth. $75.

Kelsen, Hans. *Peace Through Law.* Chapel Hill: The University of North Carolina Press, 1944. xii, 155 pp. Reprinted 2001 by The

Lawbook Exchange, Ltd. ISBN 1-58477-103-8. Cloth. $60.

Kelsen, Hans. *The Pure Theory of Law.* Translation from the Second German Edition by Max Knight. Berkeley: University of California Press, 1967. x, 356pp. Reprint available 2002 by The Lawbook Exchange, Ltd. ISBN 1-58477-206-9. Cloth. $95.

Kelsen, Hans. *Society and Nature: A Sociological Inquiry.* London: K. Kegan Paul, Trench, Trubner & Co., Ltd., [1946]. viii, 391 pp. Reprinted 2000 by The Lawbook Exchange, Ltd. LCCN 99-054869. ISBN 1-58477-064-3. Cloth. $85.

Kelsen, Hans. *What is Justice? Justice, Law and Politics in the Mirror of Science.* Berkeley: University of California Press, 1957. [vi], 397 pp. Reprinted 2000 by The Lawbook Exchange, Ltd. ISBN 1-58477-101-1. Cloth. $95.

Lieber, Francis. *Legal and Political Hermeneutics, or Principles of Interpretation and Construction in Law and Politics, with Remarks on Precedents and Authorities.* Enlarged Edition. Boston: Charles C. Little and James Brown, 1839. xii, [13]-240 pp. Reprint available 2002 by The Lawbook Exchange, Ltd. ISBN 1-58477-226-3. Cloth. $65.

Llewellyn, Karl N. *Jurisprudence. Realism in Theory and Practice.* [Chicago]: The University of Chicago Press, 1962. viii, 531 pp. Reprinted 2000 by The Lawbook Exchange, Ltd. LCCN 99-056923. ISBN 1-58477-067-8. Cloth. $95.

Mill, John Stuart. *On Liberty.* London: John W. Parker and Son, 1859. Reprint available 2002 by The Lawbook Exchange, Ltd. ISBN 1-58477-221-2. Cloth. $65.

Phillimore, John George. *Principles and Maxims of Jurisprudence.* London: John W. Parker and Son, 1856. xxiv, 408 pp. Reprinted 2001 by The Lawbook Exchange, Ltd. ISBN 1-58477-177-1. Cloth. $85.

Pollock, Sir Frederick. *The Expansion of the Common Law.* London: Stevens and Sons, Limited, 1904. vii, 164pp. Reprint available 2002 by The Lawbook Exchange, Ltd. LCCN 00-067015. ISBN 1-58477-169-0. Cloth. $65.

Pollock, Sir Frederick. *The Genius of the Common Law.* New York: The Columbia University Press, 1912. vii, 141 pp. Reprinted 2000 by The Lawbook Exchange, Ltd. LCCN 99-047160. ISBN 1-58477-043-0-1. Cloth. $55.

Pound, Roscoe. *Jurisprudence.* St. Paul, Minn.: West Publishing Co., 1959. Five volumes. Reprinted 2000 by The Lawbook Exchange, Ltd. ISBN 1-58477-119-4. Cloth. $495.

Radin, Max. *Law as Logic and Experience.* New Haven: Yale University Press, 1940. ix, [1], 171 pp. Reprinted 2000 by The Lawbook Exchange, Ltd. LCCN 99-30670. ISBN 1-58477-008-2. Cloth. $55.

Sidney, Algernon. *Discourses on Government. To which is Added, An Account of the Author's Life, and a Copious Index.* New York: Richard Lee, 1805. Three volumes. Reprint available 2002 by The Lawbook Exchange, Ltd. LCCN 2001038948. ISBN 1-58477-209-3. Cloth. $250.

Spooner, Lysander. *An Essay on the Trial by Jury.* Boston: Bela Marsh, 1852. 224 pp. Reprint available 2002 by The Lawbook Exchange, Ltd. LCCN 00-058811. ISBN 1-58477-156-9. Cloth. $70.

Stammler, Rudolph. *The Theory of Justice.* Translated by Isaak Husik. New York: The Macmillan Company, 1925. xli, 591 pp. Reprinted 2000 by The Lawbook Exchange, Ltd. LCCN 99-054019. ISBN 1-58477-066-X. Cloth. $95.

Stone, Harlan F. *Law and its Administration.* New York: Columbia University Press, 1915. vii, 232 pp. Reprint available 2002 by The Lawbook Exchange, Ltd. LCCN 00-021508. ISBN 1-58477-093-7. Cloth. $70.

Vinogradoff, Sir Paul. *Outlines of Historical Jurisprudence.* London: Oxford University Press, 1920. Two volumes. 428; x, 315 pp. Reprinted 1999 by The Lawbook Exchange, Ltd. LCCN 98-42298. ISBN 1-886363-64-1. Cloth. $150.

Walker, James. *The Theory of the Common Law.* Boston: Little, Brown and Co., 1852. xxiv, 130pp. Reprinted 1998 by The Lawbook Exchange, Ltd. LCCN 98-9522. ISBN 1-886363-45-5. Cloth. $65.

LAW AND LITERATURE

A'Beckett, Gilbert Abbott. *The Comic Blackstone* **[bound with] [Anstey, John].** *The Pleader's Guide, A Didactic Poem by John Surrebutter; American edition by James L. High.* With illustrations by George Cruikshank. Chicago: Callaghan & Cockcroft, 1870. xii, 376, 57, 65 pp. Reprinted 2001 by The Lawbook Exchange, Ltd. ISBN 1-58477-104-6. Cloth. $95.

Barton, Dunbar Plunket. *Shakespeare and the Law.* With a foreword by James M. Beck. Boston: Houghton Mifflin Company, 1929. xl, 167 pp. Reprinted 1999 by The Lawbook Exchange, Ltd. LCCN 99-26602. ISBN 1-58477-000-7. Cloth. $60.

Brown, Basil. *Law Sports at Gray's Inn (1594) Including Shakespeare's connection with the Inns of Court, the origin of the Capias Utlegatum re Coke and Bacon, Francis Bacon's connection with Warwickshire, together with a reprint of the Gesta Grayorum.* New York: [Privately Printed by the Author], 1921. xciv, 188, 88, [9] pp. LCCN 99-049829. ISBN 1-58477-056-2. Reprinted 2002 by The Lawbook Exchange, Ltd. Cloth. $85.

Campbell, John, Baron. *Shakespeare's Legal Acquirements Considered.* London: John Murray, 1859. vi, 117 pp. Reprinted 2001 by The Lawbook Exchange, Ltd. ISBN 1-58477-126-7. Cloth. $60.

Darrow, Clarence. *A Persian Pearl. And Other Essays.* East Aurora, NY: The Roycroft Shop, 1899. 175 pp. Reprinted 1997 by The Lawbook Exchange, Ltd. LCCN 97-5174. ISBN 1-886363-27-7. Cloth. $50.

Darrow, Clarence S. *An Eye for an Eye.* New York: Fox Duffield & Company, 1905. 213 pp. Reprinted 1996 by The Lawbook Exchange, Ltd. LCCN 99-047232. ISBN 1-886363-07-2. Cloth. $55.

Davis, C.K. *The Law in Shakespeare.* Washington, D.C.: Washington Law Book Co., [1883]. 303 pp. Reprinted 1999 by The Lawbook Exchange, Ltd. LCCN 98-32333. ISBN 1-886363-75-7. Cloth. $60.

Gest, John Marshall. *The Lawyer in Literature.* London: Sweet & Maxwell, Limited, 1913. xii, 249 pp. Reprinted 1999 by The Lawbook Exchange, Ltd. LCCN 99-18365. ISBN 1-886363-90-0. Cloth. $60.

Holdsworth, William S. *Charles Dickens as a Legal Historian.* New Haven: Yale University Press, 1929. 157 pp. Reprinted 1995 by The Lawbook Exchange, Ltd. LCCN 96-46579. ISBN 1-886363-06-4. Cloth. $40.

Jaques,E.T. *Charles Dickens in Chancery: Being an Account of his Proceedings in Respect of the "Christmas Carol" with Some Gossip in Relation to the Old Law Courts at Westminster.* London: Longmans, Green & Company, 1914. 95 pp. Reprinted 2001 by The Lawbook Exchange, Ltd. ISBN 1-58477-106-2. Cloth. $60.

Lockwood, Frank. *The Law and Lawyers of Pickwick.* London: The Roxburghe Press, [1910?] 108 pp. Reprint available 2002 by The

Lawbook Exchange, Ltd. ISBN 1-58477-231-X. Cloth. $55.

Neely, Robert D. *The Lawyers of Dickens and Their Clerks.* Boston: The Christopher Publishing House, [1936]. 67pp. Reprint available 2002 by The Lawbook Exchange, Ltd. LCCN 00-021520. ISBN 1-58477-091-0. Cloth. $60.

Phelps, Charles E. *Falstaff and Equity: An Interpretation.* Boston: Houghton, Mifflin and Company, 1902. xvi, 201 pp. Reprint available 2002 by The Lawbook Exchange, Ltd. ISBN 1-58477-230-1. Cloth. $65.

Valmaer. [pseud]. [Ream, Michael]. *Lawyer's Code of Ethics. A Satire.* St. Louis: The F.H. Thomas Law Book Co., 1887. 143 pp. Reprinted 2001 by The Lawbook Exchange, Ltd. LCCN 00-021508. ISBN 1-58477-047-3. Cloth. $65.

LEGAL EDUCATION

Hicks, Frederick C. *History of the Yale Law School to 1915.* With a new introduction by Morris L. Cohen and a new index. New Haven: Yale University Press, 1935-1938. 301 pp. Illustrated. Reprinted 2001 by The Lawbook Exchange, Ltd. LCCN 2001016436. ISBN 1-58477-175-5. Cloth. $75.

Hilliard, Francis. *The Elements of Law; Being a Comprehensive Summary of American Civil Jurisprudence. For the Use of Students, Men of Business, and General Readers.* Boston: Hilliard, Gray, and Company, 1835. xv, 345, v pp. Reprint available 2002 by The Lawbook Exchange, Ltd. LCCN 2001041395. ISBN 1-58477-188-7. Cloth. $75.

Kalman, Laura. *Legal Realism at Yale, 1927-1960.* Chapel Hill: University of North Carolina Press, 1986. xii, 314 pp. Reprint available 2002 by The Lawbook Exchange, Ltd. ISBN 1-58477-203-4. Cloth. $85.

Kilbourn, Dwight C. *The Bench and Bar of Litchfield County, Connecticut 1709-1909: Biographical Sketches of Members. History and Catalogue of the Litchfield Law School. Historical Notes.* Litchfield, Conn.: Published by the Author, 1909. xiv, 344, [3], viii pp. Illustrated. Reprint available 2002 by The Lawbook Exchange, Ltd. LCCN 2001038974. ISBN 1-58477-213-1. Cloth. $80.

Langdell, C.C. *A Selection of Cases on the Law of Contracts. With References and Citations. Prepared for Use as a Text-book in Harvard Law School.* Boston: Little, Brown & Co., 1871. xvi, 1022 pp. Reprinted

1999 by The Lawbook Exchange, Ltd. LCCN 99-28293. ISBN 1-58477-001-5. Cloth. $120.

Lieber, Francis. *On Civil Liberty and Self-government. Enlarged edition in one volume.* Philadelphia: J.B. Lippincott & Co.. 1859. xix, [15]-629 pp. Reprinted 2001 by The Lawbook Exchange, Ltd. LCCN 99-056928. ISBN 1-58477-070-8. Cloth. $100.

[St. Germain, Christopher]. *The Doctor and Student or Dialogues Between a Doctor of Divinity and a Student in the Laws of England Containing the Grounds of Those Laws Together with Questions and Cases Concerning the Equity Thereof Revised and Corrected by William Muchall, Gent. to which are added two pieces concerning Suits in Chancery by Subpoena.* Cincinnati: Robert Clarke & Co., 1874. xiv, 401 pp. Reprinted 1998 by The Lawbook Exchange, Ltd. LCCN 98-11338. ISBN 1-886363-49-8. Cloth. $65.

Stevens, Robert. *Law School: Legal Education in America from the 1850s to the 1980s.*Chapel Hill: The University of North Carolina Press, [1983]. xvi, 334 pp. Reprinted 2001 by The Lawbook Exchange, Ltd. ISBN 1-58477-199-2. Cloth. $85.

Walker, Timothy. *Introduction to American Law. Designed as a First Book for Students.* Ninth Edition. Revised by Clement Bates. Boston: Little, Brown, and Company, 1887. Reprint available 2002 by The Lawbook Exchange, Ltd. LCCN 2001038955. ISBN 1-58477-214-X. Cloth. $120.

Warren, Charles. *History of the Harvard Law School and of Early Legal Conditions in America.* New York: Lewis Publishing Company, 1908. Three volumes. xiv, 543; iv, 560; 397 pp. Illustrated. Reprinted 1999 by The Lawbook Exchange, Ltd. LCCN 99-29193. ISBN 1-58477-006-6. Cloth. $275.

RACE AND THE LAW

Finkelman, Paul. *An Imperfect Union: Slavery, Federalism and Comity.* Chapel Hill: The University of North Carolina Press, 1981. xii, 378 pp. Reprinted 2000 by The Lawbook Exchange, Ltd. LCCN 00-021509. ISBN 1-58477-092-9. Cloth. $85.

Finkelman, Paul. *Slavery in the Courtroom. An Annotated Bibliography of American Cases.* Washington:Library of Congress, 1985. Illustrated. xxvii, 312pp. Reprinted 1998 by The Lawbook Exchange, Ltd. LCCN 98-11284. ISBN 1-886363-48-X. Cloth. $85.

Mangum, Charles. *The Legal Status of the Negro.* New York: D. Appleton-Century Co., [1939]. xi, 354 pp. Reprinted 2000 by The Lawbook Exchange, Ltd. LCCN 99-056927. ISBN 1-58477-081-3. Cloth. $80.

Schwarz, Philip J. *Twice Condemned: Slaves and the Criminal Laws of Virginia, 1705-1865.* [Baton Rouge: Louisiana State University Press]. [1988]. xvi, 354pp. Reprinted 1998 by The Lawbook Exchange, Ltd. LCCN 98-4424 ISBN 1-886363-54-4. Cloth. $75.

U.S. STATES' RIGHTS

Minor, Raleigh C. *Notes on the Science of Government and the Relations of the States to the United States.* [Charlottesville]: University of Virginia, 1913. x, 171 pp. Reprinted 1995 by The Lawbook Exchange, Ltd. LCCN 99-047233. ISBN 1-886363-09-9. Cloth. $40.

Scott, James Brown. *Judicial Settlement of Controversies between States of the American Union: An Analysis of Cases Decided in the Supreme Court of the United States.* Oxford: Clarendon Press, 1919. xiii, 548 pp. Reprint available 2002 by The Lawbook Exchange, Ltd. LCCN 00-066333. ISBN 1-58477-172-0. Cloth. $120.

Taylor, John. *Construction Construed and Constitutions Vindicated.* Richmond: printed by Shepherd & Pollard, 1820. iv, 344pp. Reprinted 1998 by The Lawbook Exchange, Ltd. LCCN 97-49411. ISBN 1-886363-43-9. Cloth. $65.

[Taylor, John]. *A Defence of the Measures of the Administration of Thomas Jefferson. By Curtius.* Washington: Samuel H. Smith, 1804. 136 pp. Reprinted 1999 by The Lawbook Exchange, Ltd. LCCN 99-24139. ISBN 1-886363-97-8. Cloth. $60.

Taylor, John. *An Inquiry into the Principles and Policy of the Government of the United States.* Fredericksburg: Green and Cady, 1814. With an introduction by Roy Franklin Nichols, Yale University Press, 1950. 562 pp. Reprinted 1998 by The Lawbook Exchange, Ltd. LCCN 98-11147. ISBN 1-886363-46-3. Cloth. $75.

Upshur, Abel Parker. *A Brief Enquiry into the True Nature Character of Our Federal Government, being a review of Judge Story's Commentaries on the Constitution of the United States. By a Virginian.* Petersburg: Printed by Edmund and Julian C. Ruffin, 1840. 132pp. Reprinted 1998 by The Lawbook Exchange, Ltd. LCCN 97-11151. ISBN 1-886363-44-7. Cloth. $45.

Wright, John S. *Citizenship Sovereignty.* Chicago: Published for American Citizens, the True Maintainers of State Sovereignty, 1864. Reprinted 1998 by The Lawbook Exchange, Ltd. LCCN 98-15940 ISBN 1-886363-55-2. Cloth. $65.

TREATISES

Beth, Loren P. *The American Theory of Church and State.* Gainesville: University of Florida Press, 1958. vii, 183 pp. Reprint available 2002 by The Lawbook Exchange, Ltd. LCCN 2001023455. ISBN 1-58477-179-8. Cloth. $65.

Black, Henry Campbell. *A Treatise on the Law of Income Taxation under Federal and State Laws.* Kansas City: Vernon Law Book Co., 1913. xlii, 403 pp. Reprint available 2002 by The Lawbook Exchange, Ltd. ISBN 1-58477-237-9. Cloth. $85.

Brackenridge, Hugh. *Law Miscellanies: Containing an Introduction to the Study of Law; notes on Blackstone's Commentaries, Shewing the Variations of the Law of Pennsylvania from the Law of England, and what Acts of Assembly Might Require to be Repealed or Modified Observations on Smith's Edition of the Laws of Pennsylvania; Strictures on Decisions of the Supreme Court of the United States, and on Certain Acts of Congress, with Some Law Cases, and a Variety of Other Matters, Chiefly Original.* Philadelphia: P. Byrne, 1814. 588 pp. Reprinted 2001 by The Lawbook Exchange, Ltd. LCCN 00-059548. ISBN 1-58477-161-5. Cloth. $100.

Elias, Gbolahan. *Explaining Constructive Trusts.* Oxford: Clarendon Press; Oxford University Press, 1990. xxii, 177 pp. Reprint available 2002 by The Lawbook Exchange, Ltd. ISBN 1-58477-208-5. Cloth. $75.

Freeman, A.C. *A Treatise of the Law of Judgments. Including All Final Determinations of the Rights of Parties in Actions or Proceedings at Law or in Equity. Revised, and Greatly Enlarged by Edward W. Tuttle.* San Francisco: Bancroft-Whitney, 1925. Three volumes. 1216; 1280; 1264 pp. Reprinted 1993 by The Lawbook Exchange, Ltd. LCCN 99-047228. ISBN 0-9630106-6-2. Cloth. $295.

Gilmore, Grant. *Security Interests in Personal Property.* Boston: Little, Brown & Company, 1965. Two volumes. xxxiv, 651; xiii, 653-1508 pp. Reprinted 1999 by The Lawbook Exchange, Ltd. LCCN 99-10258. ISBN 1-886363-81-1. Cloth. $195.

Gould, James. *A Treatise on the Principles of Pleading in Civil Action.* Boston: Lilly and Wait, 1832. x, 536 pp. Reprint available 2002 by

The Lawbook Exchange, Ltd. LCCN 00-059549. ISBN 1-58477-158-5. Cloth. $95.

Greenleaf, Simon. *A Treatise on the Law of Evidence.* Boston: Little, Brown, and Company, 1899. Three volumes. Reprinted 2001 by The Lawbook Exchange, Ltd. LCCN 00-065554. ISBN 1-58477-116-X. Cloth. $350.

Hurst, James Willard. *Law and Markets in United States History: Different Modes of Bargaining among Interests.* [Madison]: The University of Wisconsin Press, [1982]. vii, 207 pp. Reprinted 2001 by The Lawbook Exchange, Ltd. LCCN 00-067116. ISBN 1-58477-136-4. Cloth. $80.

Laussat, Antony. *An Essay on Equity in Pennsylvania.* Philadelphia: Published for the Institution, by Robert Desilver, 1826. vi, [7]-157, [2] pp. Reprint available 2002 by The Lawbook Exchange, Ltd. LCCN 00-067115. ISBN 1-58477-139-9. Cloth. $60.

Lieber, Francis. *On Civil Liberty and Self-government. Enlarged edition in one volume.* Philadelphia: J.B. Lippincott & Co.. 1859. xix, [15]-629 pp. Reprinted 2001 by The Lawbook Exchange, Ltd. LCCN 99-056928. ISBN 1-58477-070-8. Cloth. $100.

Pothier,R.J. *Treatise on the Contract of Sale.* Translated from the French by L.S. Cushing. Boston: Charles C. Little and James Brown, 1839. xvi, 406 pp. Reprinted 2000 by The Lawbook Exchange, Ltd. LCCN 99-10260. ISBN 1-886363-82-X. Cloth. $70.

Pothier, Robert Joseph. *A Treatise on the Law of Obligations, or Contracts. Translated from the French, with an Introduction, Appendix, and Notes, Illustrative of the English Law on the Subject. By William David Evans.* London: A. Strahan, 1802. Two volumes. [1], 578, [1]; iv, 715, [1]pp. Reprinted 2000 by The Lawbook Exchange, Ltd. LCCN 99-26397. ISBN 1-886363-98-6. Cloth. $195.

Pothier, Robert Joseph. *A Treatise on Obligations, Considered in a Moral and Legal View. Translated from the French of Pothier. Translated by Francois-Xavier Martin.* Newburn, N.C.: Martin & Ogden, 1802. 2 vols. in 1 book. Reprinted 2000 by The Lawbook Exchange, Ltd. With a new introduction by Warren M. Billings. LCCN 98-38360. ISBN 1-886363-62-5. Cloth. $75.

Rogers, Edward S. *Good Will Trade-Marks and Unfair Trading.* Chicago: A.W. Shaw Company, [1914]. 288 pp. Reprint available 2002 by The Lawbook Exchange, Ltd. LCCN 2001045971. ISBN 1-58477-211-5. Cloth. $70.

Sears, John H. *Trust Estates as Business Companies.* [*Second Edition*]. Kansas City, Mo.: Vernon Law Book Company, 1921. xx, 782 pp.

[1921]. Reprinted 1998 by The Lawbook Exchange, Ltd. LCCN 97-32423 ISBN 1-886363-41-2. Cloth. $95.

Story, Joseph. *Commentaries on the Conflict of Laws, Foreign and Domestic, in Regard to Contracts, Rights, and Remedies, and Especially in Regard to Marriages, Divorces, Wills, Successions, and Judgments. Second Edition. Revised, Corrected and Greatly Enlarged.* London: A. Maxwell, 1841. xxxiv, 927 pp. (misnumbered in original, PP. 753-756 omitted.) Reprinted 2001 by The Lawbook Exchange, Ltd. ISBN 1-58477-145-3. Cloth. $125.

Tiedeman, Christopher G. *A Treatise on State and Federal Control of Persons and Property in the United States Considered from both a Civil and Criminal Standpoint.* St. Louis: The F.H. Thomas Law Book Co., 1900. Two volumes. Reprint available 2002 by The Lawbook Exchange, Ltd. ISBN 1-58477-229-8. Cloth. $195.

Wheaton, Henry. *Elements of International Law: with a Sketch of the History of the Science.* Philadelphia: Carey, Lea & Blanchard, 1836. xiv, 375 pp. Reprint available 2002 by The Lawbook Exchange, Ltd. LCCN 00-066335. ISBN 1-58477-170-4. Cloth. $80.

Wiener, Frederick Bernays. *Briefing and Arguing Federal Appeals.* xvi, 506 pp. Washington, D.C.: BNA Incorporated, 1961. xvi, 506 pp. Reprinted with a new introduction by Bryan A. Garner. Reprinted 2001 by The Lawbook Exchange, Ltd. LCCN 2001031682. ISBN 1-58477-183-6. Cloth. $85.

Wrightington, Sydney R. *The Law of Unincorporated Associations and Similar Relations.* Boston: Little, Brown, and Company, 1916. xxvi, 486 pp. Reprint available 2002 by The Lawbook Exchange, Ltd. LCCN 2001045970. ISBN 1-58477-205-0. Cloth. $125.

UNITED STATES CONSTITUTIONAL LAW

Adams, John. *A Defence of the Constitutions of Government of the United States of America.* Philadelphia: Printed by Budd and Bartram, for William Corbett, 1797. Three volumes. Reprinted 2001 by The Lawbook Exchange, Ltd. LCCN 00-067586. ISBN 1-58477-140-2. Cloth. $250.

Baldwin, Henry. *A General View of the Origin and Nature of the Constitution and Government of the United States, Deduced from the Political History and Condition of the Colonies and States, from 1774 until 1788. And the Decisions of the Supreme Court of the United States. Together with Opinions in the Cases Decided at January Term, 1837, Arising on the Restraints on the Powers of the States.* Philadelphia,

Printed by J. C. Clark, 1837. v, [1], 197 p. Reprinted 2000 by The Lawbook Exchange, Ltd. LCCN 00-026728. ISBN 1-58477-098-8. Cloth. $60.

Bancroft, George. *History of the Formation of the Constitution of the United States of America. Second Edition.* New York: D. Appleton and Company, 1882. Two volumes. xxiv, 520; xiv,501 pp. Reprinted 2000 by The Lawbook Exchange, Ltd. LCCN 99-23946. ISBN 1-58477-002-3. Cloth. $175.

Bauer, Elizabeth Kelley. *Commentaries on the Constitution 1790-1860.* New York: Columbia University Press, 1952. 400 pp. Reprinted 1999 by The Lawbook Exchange, Ltd. LCCN 98-45409. ISBN 1-886363-66-8. Cloth. $75.

Beard, Charles. *An Economic Interpretation of the Constitution of the United States.* New York: The Macmillan Company, 1952. xxi, 330 pp. Reprinted 2001 by The Lawbook Exchange, Ltd. LCCN 00-036834. ISBN 1-58477-111-9. Cloth. $80.

Beard, Charles A. *The Supreme Court and the Constitution.* New York: The Macmillan Company, 1912. vii, 127 pp. Reprinted 1999 by The Lawbook Exchange, Ltd. LCCN 98-50368. ISBN 1-886363-78-1. Cloth. $45.

Bondy, William. *Separation of Governmental Powers in History, in Theory, and in the Constitutions.* New York: Columbia College, 1896. Reprinted 1999 by The Lawbook Exchange, Ltd. vi,[7]-185, [1] pp. LCCN 98-44994. ISBN 1-886363-65-X. Cloth. $65.

Brown, Everett S. *The Constitutional History of the Louisiana Purchase 1803-1812.* Berkeley: University of California Press, 1920. xi, 248 pp. Reprinted 2001 by The Lawbook Exchange, Ltd. ISBN 1-58477-151-8. Cloth. $75.

Calhoun, John C. *A Disquisition on Government and a Discourse on the Constitution and Government of the United States.* Edited by Richard K. Cralle. Charleston, S.C.: Steam Power-Press of Walker and James, 1851. viii, 406 pp. Reprint available 2002 by The Lawbook Exchange, Ltd. LCCN 00-067584. ISBN 1-58477-127-5. Cloth. $80.

Chipman, Nathaniel. *Principles of Government. A Treatise on Free Institutions Including the Constitution of the United States.* Burlington: Edward Smith, 1833. viii, 144, 145a-188a, [145]-330 pp. Reprinted 2001 by The Lawbook Exchange, Ltd. LCCN 99-048863. ISBN 1-58477-046-5. Cloth. $80.

Cohn, Morris M. *An Introduction to the Study of the Constitution; A Study showing the Play of Physical and Social Factors in the Creation of Institutional Law.* Baltimore: The Johns Hopkins Press, 1892. xi, 235 pp. Reprinted 2000 by The Lawbook Exchange, Ltd. LCCN 99-38730. ISBN 1-58477-032-5. Cloth. $50.

Cooley, Thomas M. *The General Principles of Constitutional Law in the United States* of America. Boston: Little, Brown, and Company, 1880. xxxix, 376 pp. Reprinted 2001 by The Lawbook Exchange, Ltd. LCCN 00-056301. ISBN 1-58477-120-8. Cloth. $85.

Cooley, Thomas McIntyre. *A Treatise on the Constitutional Limitations Which Rest Upon the Legislative Power of the States of the American Union. [1st edition].* Boston: Little, Brown, and Co., 1868. xlvii, 720pp. Reprinted 1999 by The Lawbook Exchange, Ltd. LCCN 99-20589. ISBN 1-886363-92-7. Cloth. $95.

Cooley, Thomas M. *A Treatise on the Constitutional Limitations which Rest Upon the Legislative Power of the States of the American Union. Fifth edition.* Boston: Little, Brown, and Co., 1883. lxxxi, 886pp. Reprinted 1998 by The Lawbook Exchange, Ltd. LCCN 98-12730. ISBN 1-886363-53-6. Cloth. $120.

Corwin, Edward. *The Doctrine of Judicial Review: Its Legal and Historical Basis and Other Essays.* Princeton: Princeton University Press, 1914. ix, 178 pp. Reprinted 2000 by The Lawbook Exchange, Ltd. LCCN 99-32362. ISBN 1-58477-011-2. Cloth. $60.

Curtis,George Ticknor and Joseph Culbertson Clayton. *Constitutional History of the United States from their Declaration of Independence to the Close of the Civil War.* New York: Harper & Brothers, 1889, 1896. Two volumes. xiii, 774; x, 780 pp. Reprint available 2002 by The Lawbook Exchange, Ltd. LCCN 00-065554. ISBN 1-58477-129-1. Cloth. $250.

Duer, William Alexander. *A Course of Lectures on the Constitutional Jurisprudence of the United States; Delivered Annually in Columbia College, New York. The Second Edition, Revised, Enlarged, and Adapted to Professional as well as General Use.* Boston: Little, Brown & Co., 1856. xxiv, 545 pp. Reprinted 2000 by The Lawbook Exchange, Ltd. LCCN 99-16385. ISBN 1-58477-020-1. Cloth. $85.

Fisher, Sydney George. *The Evolution of the Constitution of the United States. Showing That It Is a Development of Progressive History and Not an Isolated Document Struck Off at a Given Time or an Imitation of English or Dutch Forms of Government.* Philadelphia: J.B. Lippincott, 1897. 398 pp. Reprinted 1996 by The Lawbook Exchange, Ltd. LCCN 97-41054. ISBN 1-886363-08-0. Cloth. $65.

Flanders, Henry. *An Exposition of the Constitution of the United States. Designed as a Manual of Instruction.* Philadelphia: E.H. Butler & Co., 1860. xii, 311 pp. Reprinted 1999 by The Lawbook Exchange, Ltd. LCCN 99-31594. ISBN 1-58477-014-7. Cloth. $60.

Ford, Paul Leicester. *Pamphlets on the Constitution of the United States, Published During Its Discussion by the People 1787-1788.* Brooklyn, N.Y., 1888. viii, 451 pp. Reprinted 2000 by The Lawbook Exchange, Ltd. LCCN 99-25089. ISBN 1-886363-95-1. Cloth. $75.

Haines, Charles Grove. *The Role of the Supreme Court in American Government and Politics 1789-1835.* Berkeley: University of California Press, 1944. xiii, 679 pp. Reprint available 2002 by The Lawbook Exchange, Ltd. ISBN 1-58477-207-7. Cloth. $120.

Haines, Charles Grove and Foster Sherwood. *The Role of the Supreme Court in American Government and Politics 1835-1869.* Berkeley: University of California Press, 1957. x, 533 pp. Reprint available 2002 by The Lawbook Exchange, Ltd. ISBN 1-58477-197-6. Cloth. $95.

Hamilton, Alexander, James Madison and John Jay]. *The Federalist: A Collection of Essays, Written in Favour of the New Constitution, As Agreed Upon by the Federal Convention, September 17, 1787.* New-York: J. and A. M'Lean, 1788. Two volumes. Reprinted 2002 by The Lawbook Exchange, Ltd. LCCN 2001037703. ISBN 1-58477-204-2. Cloth. $295.

Henderson, Gerard Carl. *The Position of Foreign Corporations in American Constitutional Law. A Contribution to the History and Theory of Juristic Persons in Anglo-American Law.* Cambridge: Harvard University Press, 1918. xix, 199 pp. Reprinted 1999 by The Lawbook Exchange, Ltd. LCCN 99-18233. ISBN 1-886363-89-7. Cloth. $50.

Lansing, John, Jr. *The Delegate from New York or Proceedings of the Federal Convention of 1787 from the Notes of John Lansing, Jr.* Edited by Joseph Reese Strayer. Princeton: Princeton University Press, 1939. x, 125 pp. Reprint available 2002 by The Lawbook Exchange, Ltd. LCCN 2001050456. ISBN 1-58477-218-2. Cloth. $60.

[Madison, James]. Hunt, Gaillard, Scott, James Brown. *The Debates in The Federal Convention of 1787 Which Framed the Constitution of the United States of America.* New York: Oxford University Press, 1920. xcvii, [1], 731 pp. Reprinted 1999 by The Lawbook Exchange, Ltd. LCCN 98-51911. ISBN 1-886363-77-3. Cloth. $110.

Marshall, John. *The Constitutional Decisions of John Marshall,* Edited, with an introductory essay by Joseph P. Cotton, Jr. New York: G.P. Putnam, 1905. Two volumes. viii, 144, 145a-188a, [145]-330 pp. Reprinted 2001 by The Lawbook Exchange, Ltd. LCCN 99-048862. ISBN 1-58477-050-3. Cloth. $175.

Mathews, John. *Legislative and Judicial History of the Fifteenth Amendment.* Originally published Baltimore: The Johns Hopkins Press, 1909. x, 11-126 pp. Reprinted 2001 by The Lawbook Exchange, Ltd. ISBN 1-58477-176-3. Cloth. $60.

McLaughlin, Andrew C. *The Foundations of American Constitutionalism.* New York: The New York University Press, 1932. vii, 176 pp. Reprint available 2002 by The Lawbook Exchange, Ltd. ISBN 1-58477-227-1. Cloth. $65.

Poore, Ben[jamin] Perley. *The Federal and State Constitutions, Colonial Charters, and Organic Laws of the United States. Second edition.* Washington: Government Printing Office, 1878. Folio, book measures 7" x 10." Two volumes. xii, 1019; 1021-2102 pp. Reprinted 2001 by The Lawbook Exchange, Ltd. ISBN 1-58477-128-3. Cloth. $395.

Powell, Edward Payson. *Nullification and Secession in the United States.* New York: G.P. Putnam's Sons, 1897. xi, 461 pp. Reprint available 2002 by The Lawbook Exchange, Ltd. LCCN 00-067013. ISBN 1-58477-132-1. Cloth. $85.

Powell, Thomas Reed. *Vagaries and Varieties in Constitutional Interpretation.* New York: Columbia University Press, 1956. xv, 229 pp. Reprint available 2002 by The Lawbook Exchange, Ltd. ISBN 1-58477-210-7. Cloth. $65.

Schofield, Henry. *Essays on Constitutional Law and Equity and Other Subjects.* Boston: The Chipman Law Publishing Company, 1921. Two volumes. Reprint available 2002 by The Lawbook Exchange, Ltd. LCCN 2001043982. ISBN 1-58477-223-9. Cloth. $195.

Scott, James Brown. *James Madison's Notes of Debates in the Federal Convention of 1787 and their Relation to a More Perfect Society of Nations.* New York: Oxford University Press, 1918. xviii, 149pp. Reprinted 2001 by The Lawbook Exchange, Ltd. ISBN 1-58477-164-X. Cloth. $65.

Scott, James Brown. *The United States of America: A Study in International Organization.* New York: Oxford University Press, 1920. xix, 605 pp. Reprint available 2002 by The Lawbook Exchange, Ltd. LCCN 00-067016. ISBN 1-58477-171-2. Cloth. $120.

Story, Joseph. *Commentaries on the Constitution of the United States.* Boston: Little, Brown and Company, 1858. Two volumes. xxxiii, 735, 702pp. Reprinted 2001 by The Lawbook Exchange, Ltd. ISBN 1-58477-193-3. Cloth. $250.

Story, Joseph. *A Familiar Exposition of the Constitution of the United States:* Containing a Brief Commentary on Every Clause, Explaining the True Nature, reasons, and Objects Thereof; Designed for the Use of School, Libraries and General Readers. With an Appendix, Containing Important Public Documents, Illustrative of the Constitution. New York: Harper & Brothers: 1865. 372 pp. Reprinted 1999 by The Lawbook Exchange, Ltd. LCCN 98-50811. ISBN 1-886363-71-4. Cloth. $60.

Taylor, John, of Caroline. *New Views of the Constitution of the United States.* Washington City: Printed for the Author, 1823. [4], 316pp. Reprint available 2002 by The Lawbook Exchange, Ltd. ISBN 1-58477-079-1. Cloth. $70.

Tiedeman, Christopher G. *A Treatise on the Limitations of Police Power in the United States Considered from both a Civil and Criminal Standpoint.* St. Louis: The F.H. Thomas Law Book Co., 1886. lxv, 662 pp. Reprinted 2001 by The Lawbook Exchange, Ltd. ISBN 1-58477-122-4. Cloth. $110.

Tucker, Henry St. George. *Commentaries on the Laws of Virginia. Comprising the Substance of a Course of Lectures Delivered to the Winchester Law School. With an Introduction by David Cobin and Paul Finkelman.* Richmond: Shepherd and Colin, 1846. Two volumes. 34, 468; 24, 512 pp. Reprinted 1998 by The Lawbook Exchange, Ltd. LCCN 97-10313. ISBN 1-886363-26-9. Cloth. $175.

Tucker, Henry St. George. *Limitations on the Treaty-Making Power Under the Constitution of the United States.* Boston: Little, Brown, and Company, 1915. xxi, 444 pp. Reprinted 2000 by The Lawbook Exchange, Ltd. LCCN 99-31589. ISBN 1-58477-015-5. Cloth. $75.

Tucker, St. George. *Blackstone's Commentaries. With Notes of Reference to the Constitution and Laws, of the Federal Government of the United States, and of the Commonwealth of Virginia. In Five Volumes, with an Appendix to Each volume, Containing Short Tracts upon Such Subjects As Appeared Necessary to Form a Connected View of the Laws of Virginia As a Member of the Federal Union.* Philadelphia: William Young Birch and Abraham Small, 1803. Five volumes. Reprinted 1996 by The Lawbook Exchange, Ltd. LCCN 96-12566. ISBN 1-886363-15-3. Cloth. $450.

Twiss, Benjamin R. *Lawyers and the Constitution: How Laissez Faire Came to the Supreme Court.* With a foreword by Edward S. Corwin.

xii, 271 pp. Princeton University Press, [1942]. Reprinted 2001 by The Lawbook Exchange, Ltd. LCCN 00-067114. ISBN 1-58477-138-0. Cloth. $75.

Vile, John, ed. *Proposed Amendments to the U.S. Constitution 1787-2001.* Three volumes. Available 2002 by The Lawbook Exchange, Ltd. ISBN 1-58477-225-5. Cloth. $450.

Whiting, William. *War Powers under the Constitution of the United States. Military Arrests, Reconstruction & Military Government. Also, Now First Published, War Claims of Aliens with Notes on the Acts of the Executives & Legislative Departments During Our Civil War & a Collection of Cases Decided in the National Courts. 1864. Tenth edition.* Boston: Little, Brown, and Company, 1864. xvii, 342 pp. Reprint available 2002 by The Lawbook Exchange, Ltd. LCCN 99-049360. ISBN 1-58477-055-4. Cloth. $80.

Willoughby, Westel W. *The Supreme Court of the United States. Its History and Influence in our Constitutional System.* Baltimore: The Johns Hopkins Press, 1890. 124 pp. Reprinted 2001 by The Lawbook Exchange, Ltd. LCCN 00-068896. ISBN 1-58477-147-X. Cloth. $60.

WOMEN AND THE LAW

Kitchin, S.B. *A History of Divorce.* London: Chapman & Hall, Ltd., 1912. xvi, 293 pp. Reprint available 2002 by The Lawbook Exchange, Ltd. LCCN 2001041400. ISBN 1-58477-190-9. Cloth. $75.

Reeve, Tapping (1744-1823). *The Law of Baron and Femme, of Parent and Child, Guardian and Ward, Master and Servant, and of the Powers of the Courts of Chancery; with an Essay on the Terms Heir, Heirs, Heirs of the Body. Third Edition, With Notes and References to English and American Cases by Amasa J. Parker and Charles E. Baldwin, Counselors-At-Law.* Albany: William Gould, 1862. xlvi, 677pp. Reprinted 1998 by The Lawbook Exchange, Ltd. LCCN 98-36057. ISBN 1-886363-58-7. Cloth. $75.

Woolsey, Theodore D. *Divorce and Divorce Legislation, Especially in the United States. Second Edition Revised.* New York: Charles Scribner's Sons, 1882. x, [9]-328 pp. Reprinted 2001 by The Lawbook Exchange, Ltd. ISBN 1-58477-118-6. Cloth. $75.